OUTLINES

OF

HEBREW ACCENTUATION,

PROSE AND POETICAL.

BY THE

Rev. A. B. DAVIDSON, M.A.

כל פירוש שאיננו על פירוש הטעמים לא תאבה לו ולא תשמע אליו
ABEN EZRA.

WILLIAMS AND NORGATE,

14, HENRIETTA STREET, COVENT GARDEN, LONDON,

AND

20, SOUTH FREDERICK STREET, EDINBURGH.

MDCCCLXI.

PREFACE.

THE following tract was undertaken to supply a want
in most Hebrew Grammars that are current,—a want
especially felt in connection with the teaching in the
New College. It has always been the practice of Dr.
Duncan, the Hebrew Professor there, to give instruc-
tion in the whole Masoretic punctual system, vowels
and accents alike. This is the natural course for a
thorough scholar to take—the course, indeed, which a
thorough scholar must take; for many parts of the
mechanism of the vocalic system cannot be understood,
without, at the same time, understanding the disturb-
ing influence of the accentual system upon it. This
natural way, however, was often practically not quite
successful, from the want of anything to which the
Student might refer when the Teacher's explanations
were forgotten or misunderstood. I thus thought that
a short tract on the question, containing the chief facts
or rules—without unnecessary attempt at *rationale*, on
a subject which some will deem wholly irrational—might
not be unwelcome to Students. To Dr. Duncan, who
urged me to undertake the thing, I am indebted directly

for the prose table, p. 53, and for much more indirectly. He is in no way responsible, however, for anything in the tract, whether statement or theory ; much less for any of the blunders. I am persuaded that had he written it there would have been no blunders in it. It is to the sad loss of learning, both in his own and all other countries, that he cannot be induced to put his own hand to something permanent.

I have treated of the poetic accents much more fully than of those of prose. The chief reason of this was that the poetic books are much more circumscribed, and I was not launched upon an infinite sea, but could see from shore to shore. I have read and scanned these books several times ; but from my want of correct Edd.—for I have not been able to purchase the dearer Edd., and libraries are shamefully destitute of them—this process has almost been useless, for conclusions formed on the practice of one Ed. have been often overturned by the practice of another. The Ed. of Michaelis, and, later, the beautiful print of Baer (on whose Hebrew tract, *Torath Emeth*, because condensed out of the native masters, I have chiefly relied), have been mostly used by me ; but I have occasionally given references to the Edd. of Theile and Hahn, because these are chiefly in the hands of Students.

So far as I know, the present tract, with the exception of Cross's Treatise, is the only separate composition on the accentual question in our language. It will be found, I fear, to contain many mistakes ; but the subject is peculiar, and the aids not very numerous; and, with all its deficiencies, I think it might contribute to some understanding of the elements of the accentual system, the understanding of which I am persuaded would contribute much to the fuller understanding and deeper feeling of the Scriptures.

Being averse to risking anything of my own on the subject, I thought first of translating Ewald's exhaustive treatise from his Lehrbuch; but, like all that author's works, it is too cunning and abstruse for beginners. Some may demur to certain of Ewald's speculations; but to him belongs the commanding merit of having first speculated. I should still like to put his treatise into an English form.

EDINBURGH,
    March, 1861.

ERRATA.

Introd. p. xv., for אם read עַם
p. 40, for מלכתו read מלאכתו

CONTENTS.

SECT		PAGE.
	INTRODUCTION	vii
1	Accent Uses	1
2	Antiquity and Authority	18
3	Accentual Signs	28
4	Interpunction	35
5	Table of Prose Accentuation	53
6	Clause of Silluq	56
7	„ Athnach	58
8	„ Sgolta	60
9	„ Zaqeph	63
10	„ Tippecha	66
11	„ Rbhia	68
12	„ Tbhir, Zarqa, and Pashta	70
13	„ Geresh, Pazer, etc.	72

POETIC ACCENTUATION

1	Poetic Accentuation	75
2	Interpunction	83
3	Metrical Table	85
4	Clause of Silluq	88
5	„ Rbhia Mugrash	95
6	„ Athnach	98
7	„ Olehveyored	101
8	„ Dechi, or Tip. Anterior	104
9	„ Zinnor or Zarqa	106
10	„ Rbhia	108
11	„ Pazer	110
12	„ Legarmeh	111

INTRODUCTION.

BUXTORF, the younger, when introducing a quarto of nearly five hundred pages on the accents and vowels, gracefully apologizes for making so much noise about the *point*, to which the children of the mathematicians deny all magnitude. Some people may think any labour bestowed upon the accents ill-spent. But, surely, no labour is ill-spent which is spent upon the text of Scripture. And it must not be forgotten that accents and vowels are of the same authority, both having sprung entire from the head of the Masorete, and whoso condemns the one condemns the other. No doubt those whose condemnation falls so ruinously upon the accents, would dispense with the vowels as well. Would many of them feel the loss of dispensing with the consonants also?

Perhaps an apology could most significantly be made by showing what sort of men have devoted themselves to this branch of inquiry.[1] And, indeed, every man in this or almost any other age, since the renascence of Hebrew learning, who has any claim to be regarded as a Hebrew scholar, has investigated the laws of the accents. Not all with equal profundity or equal success, but all in one way or other have given some, and

[1] Quanto interessante, altrettanto poco o male coltivato ramo—as Luzzatto musically mourns. Gramm., p. 75.

many much, thought to the question. The man who stands at the head of Hebrew grammarians at this moment, Ewald of Gœttingen, so far from thinking the matter unworthy of his mind, has returned to it from time to time from his youth up to the present date.[2] Hupfeld, who stands next to him, and, as an investigator of Jewish sources, before him, has written at divers times and in many ways on the topic.[3] Luzzatto, the great Rabbin of Padua, thinks the subject not unworthy of being discussed in the music of his native tongue.[4] Even America makes herself heard on the question.[5] Jews[6] and Christians alike pour in their contributions.

[2] His early essay on the subject in Abhandlungen zur Orient. u. Bibl. Litteratur, Erster Theil, 1832, p. 130 fol. The same vol. contains a valuable essay on the Syriac punctuation, after Syriac MSS., s. 53 folg. Also Die Assyrisch-hebraische punctation, Jahrbucher der Bib. Wissenschaft Erstes Jahrbuch, 1848, s. 160. His maturer views in the exhaustive treatise in his Ausfuhr. Lehrbuch der Heb. Sprache, p. 160–217, Gœttingen, 1855. (On the Syriac *metre*, see Hahn, Bardesanes Gnosticus, etc, and his Syr. Chrestomathy. Also Burgess, Metrical Hymns, etc. Introduction. On the Arabic, Ewald's Gram. Arab. Appendix.

[3] Beleuchtung dunkler Stellen der alttest. Textgeschichte, Stud. u Krit., 1830 and 1837. Also Ausfuhrliche Heb. Grammatik. s. 84 ff, and especially s. 115 ff. Cassel, 1841.—Commentatio de antiquioribus apud Judæos accentuum Scriptoribus, part i. Hahs, 1846, part ii, ibid. 1847. —De rei grammaticæ ap. Jud. initis. Hal., 1846. And the remarkable essay, Das zwiefache Grundgesetz des Rhythmus u. Accents, od. das Verhaltniss des rhythmischen zum logischen Princip der menschlichen Sprachmelodie, Zeitsch. der Deutsch. Morgenland Gesellschaft. Sechster Band, p. 153 (1852),

[4] In his Grammatica della Lingua Ebraica, fasc i, p 47–75, promising also much more at the end of this work, which has not yet come, Padova, 1853-7. Also in his valuable מכתב to Baer, at the end of Torath Emeth of the latter. Prolegomeni ad una Grammatica ragionata della Ling Ebr., and the periodical כרם חמר, vol vii, cited in his Grammar.

[5] Nordheimer's Heb. Grammar, 2 vols, New York, 1838, containing a fair, though by no means complete treatise on the accents.

[6] S. Baer. (תורת אמת (רב), an exhaustive treatise on the poetical accents.—The numerous works of Leop. Dukes.—G. J. Polak, the editor of Ben Bilam.—H. Philipowski, his annotator, and editor of Menachem Ben Saruq.—Wolf Heidenheim (d. h. aus Heidenheim) ספר משפטי הטעמים, a great work on the prose accents, collected from the Masorah and the old masters. All my efforts have failed to procure this

In the last century and century foregoing, Germans,[7] Dutchmen,[8] Swiss,[9] Englishmen,[10] Scotchmen,[11] even

book, which I much regret. It is rare. Steinschneider in his Bibliographisches Handbuch calls it sehr geschatzt u selten It was printed at Rodelheim, 1808 Heidenheim composed a similar treatise on the poetic accents, which has never been printed. Dukes (Beitrage 3 Bändchen, s. 194), informs us that it is, still extant, and in the hands of a certain Mr Lehren in Amsterdam, מִי יִתֵּן וְיֹצִיאֵהוּ לָאוֹר ' Heidenheim has given a number of his results in his preface to his edition of the Psalter So Baer in his Psalter has furnished a very brief outline of the poetic system.—To these must be added the works of Fürst, Zunz, Delitzsch, and many more The latter has furnished some interesting details in the second vol of his Commentary on the Psalms, and paid much attention to the accentuation throughout his Commentary.

[7] For example, Ad Bened Spitzner, Institutiones ad Analyticam Sacram Textus Heb V T ex accentibus. Halis, 1786; a work of which Hupfeld says, that both philosophically and practically, it is the first of all accentual treatises —Michaelis, in his notes to his Bible, has paid great attention to the accents, the whole lower margin of his Ed is devoted to a collation of MSS and discussions of the best readings He has introduced many amendments, though some of the principles on which he proceeded have been found to be wrong.

[8] Philip Ouseel, M.D Introductio in accentuationem Heb. 2 vols 4to. Lug Bat (the poetical, 1714; the prose, 1715) A very valuable treatise, especially as exhibiting a vast number of examples In some respects wrong and superseded

[9] The works of the Buxtorfs, elder and younger That of the latter very valuable, Tractatus de punct. vocal et acc in lib vet test heb origine, antiquitate, et authoritate Basil. 1648 —(Other works, see below, p 20, note 4)

[10] Walter Cross, the Taghmical (טעם) Art, or the art of expounding Scripture by the points usually called accents. London, 1698 Acute and amusing Seems to have been used by Boston It does not appear to what profession Cross belonged : he was an M A, and confesses to having sometimes preached '

[11] Thomas Boston, of Ettrick. Thomæ Boston, ecclesiæ atricensis apud Scotos pastoris, Tractatus Stigmologicus Hebræo-Biblicus Amstelodami, 1738 Boston's sorrows, from the accents and other less serious annoyances, may be read in his pathetic memoirs. No doubt they had much to do with that "notable breach in his health," of which he complains. He seems first of all to have written his work in English and then turned it into Latin, an English copy having been found among his papers And, indeed, the Latin itself shows sufficiently how it arose. Another learned Scotchman who wrote on the accents and points was Robertson, author of the Clavis Pentateuchi, etc Edinburgh, 1770

The works mentioned in the above notes are, with the two or three native tracts to be mentioned immediately, the chief aids used in compiling the following tract The literature of the accents has been exhausted in a

Presbyterian Ministers thought the doctrine of the
accents not beneath their notice, and its study not in-
compatible with the severe gravity and practical duty
which their Church demands of them.

More important often than the speculations of Chris-
tian grammarians are the hints contained in the Masorah,
which frequently lays down positive laws on particular
usages, and enumerates the occurrences of peculiar
combinations These laws and observances, so far as
they are intelligible, must be considered as general
principles, and Edd. corrected in conformity with them.
The Masorah, however, is so confused and unintelligible
that not much that is rational can be drawn from its
depths ; and, except some devoted Jewish inquirers, few
have the courage to let themselves down into its un-
illumined abysses.

Of an importance only second to the Masorah, are the
deductions of early native investigators, who stood so
near the authoritative age as to be almost able to hear
its voices; though, unfortunately, what we have from
remoter eras has fallen into such a state of confusion
through repeated and ignorant transcription, that in
many cases it cannot be understood, and in most others,
where it can be understood, it cannot be believed. The
greater part of what the earliest investigators have left
us, has found editors and expositors in the grammarians
of the present day, Ewald, Hupfeld, Delitzsch, Dukes,
etc. The first[12] native accentuists were Ben Asher,

note by Delitzsch to his Commentary on the Psalms, ii , s 520 ff, to
which those who wish more names are referred. The majority of the
works there alluded to are antiquated, and, with the exception of *Wasmuth*,
superseded ; the attainments of their authors have been far exceeded by
the writers named above.

[12] Etheridge, indeed, in his Heb. Literature, p 206, mentions a work,

Chayyug, and Ben Bilam; and as these names are un-
familiar to our English tongue, a brief account of them
and their works in this department may be tolerated.

It is evident, at least, that such a man as Aharon Ben
Asher lived, and that he wrote on the points. (1). He
is frequently cited by Jewish writers, *e.g.* Qimchi.[13]
(2). A long list, amounting to 864 particulars—more
numerous according to Walton—is circulated, in which
he disagreed with Ben Naphtali, representing on his
side the Western, while Naphtali represented the Eastern
recension of the Jewish Scriptures.[14] It is to be ob-
served, however, that the differences of these critics are
not confined exclusively to particulars, but embrace also
principles,[15] and thus they may be regarded as bringing
up the long train of authorities, their successors content-
ing themselves with copying, but inventing or deciding
nothing.[16] Dukes supposes that these particulars must
have come from the hand of Ben Asher himself, and that
later scholars copied them out and cited them as well as
those of his opponent. (3). All are agreed that Ben Asher
was greatly versed in accentual and vocalic lore; that

Horayath haq-Q'ri, by an unknown author, prior to the 11th century, who
wrote in Arabic. He says it was translated into Heb. by Menachem ben
Nathaniel, and exists in MS. in the Vatican. Whether the MS be of
the original or of the translation he does not say, nor does he quote any
writer who cites the work, nor any writer to whom he himself is indebted
for his information Ben Bilam wrote a tract of a similar name, and him-
self cites it in a later work on the same subject (see below). This later
work is extant in several libraries, among others, the Vatican, under the
former name, viz , *Hor haq-Qōrē*.

[13] Book of Roots. R עֲנָי. Commentary on Judges "כ"ו Dukes,
Qonteres, p 4 Buxtorf, Tract punct , p 262 ff.

[14] Bleek, Einleitung, s 737, 807 De Wette (Parker), i 360 Eich-
horn Einl , i 376, ii 698 Jud Lit in Ersch and Gruber , s 414

[15] For example, Naphtali adheres to the rule, disregarded entirely by
Ben Asher, that only *one* accent should be allowed on one word Baer in
Del ii., notes, pp. 460, 462, 465

[16] Eichhorn, i 370. Hupf Commentatio i , note 8

he spent many years in correcting a copy of the Scrip-
tures after authoritative MSS., which copy was con-
sidered highly valuable, and was kept for purposes of
transcription both in Jerusalem and Egypt, being often
copied, as, for instance, by Maimonides.[17]   (4). His
name is prefixed to some disjointed observations on the
accents, both prose and poetical, first published at the
end of the Rabbinical Bible, Venice, 1517 ; and in a
corrected form, inserted in the final Masorah by Ben
Chayim, in the revised edition of that Bible, 1526.   The
chief parts of these remarks were published separately
by Hupfeld,[18] and again in a fuller and considerably
different form, from a MS. in the hands of Luzzatto, by
Leop. Dukes, with preface and notes in Hebrew.[19]   Both
the editor and Luzzatto are of opinion that the two re-
censions have proceeded from the author's own hand, just
as two recensions of Ben Bilam's treatise originated im-
mediately with him, and one is quoted by him in the
other.

Neither is there much difficulty in fixing the period
at which Ben Asher flourished, nor the school which
was the scene of his labours.   (1). The fragment pub-
lished in the Venetian Bible under his name introduces
itself by saying—This is the book on the subtleties
(Grammar)[20] of the accents, composed by Rab. Aharon

---

[17] Bleek, Einl , s. 808.   Eichhorn, i 374   The words of Maimonides
in Buxtorf, Tractatus, p. 273.

[18] Commentatio, ut sup. Appendix i   Also the poetical frag. by Polak
at the end of Ben Bilam , and by Heidenheim, pref. to his Psalter.

[19] Under the title אשר לבן המיוחס המסורת קונטרס.   Also with
German title, Kontres hammasoreth, angeblich von Ben Ascher   Tü-
bingen, 1846   See also Beitrage zur Gesch. der altest. Auslegung u s.
w. des Alten Test   Stuttgart, 1844.   Von Ewald-Dukes, Zweites Band.
(von Dukes), s. 120 annu.

[20] הט" מדקדוקי ספר זה.   The derivatives from the root דק are used
with this signification, e g. דקדוק grammar, מדקדק grammarian.

ben Asher, מִמְקוֹם מֵעֲזִיָה, which is called *Tiberias* upon
the sea of Genneseret. This superscription expresses,
at least, the general tradition regarding Ben Asher.
The word מֵעֲזִיָה is very enigmatical.[21] (2). The fact
that his readings were current in the West, and adhered
to by the Western Jews, shews that the sphere of his
influence was in the West.[22] (3) The period assigned
to him by R. Gedaliah is 794, that is 1034 of our era,
and with this date most authorities agree.[23] It may
thus be assumed that he was of the school of Tiberias.
and belonged to the early part of the 11th century.

What are the probabilities that this fragment on the
accents is due to him? (1). There is the express
declaration of the fragment itself. (2). Its great
antiquity, for Dukes asserts that the earliest accentuists.
such as Ben Bilam; R. Yequtiel han-Naqdan, author
of עֵין הַקּוֹרֵא; and Mosheh han-Naqdan, author of
ס' הַנִּקּוּד, have made great use of it.[24] The antiquity
of the tract is further proved from its language,
which, in addition to being excessively obscure[25] and
full of conceits, is, in the first place, exclusively
Hebrew, with no intermixture of Chaldee, indicating a
time soon after the renascence of the native Palestinian
speech; and, in the second place, in the form of rhymes,

[21] See the speculations of Hupf. and others regarding it, in his Com-
mentatio, part i., p. 4, note 8

[22] See quotations regarding his influence, Buxtorf, Tract., p. 264 ff
He is generally, however, believed to have lived and taught in Babylonia
Bartolocci says of him and B. Naphtali—uterque floruit in Babylonia circ
1034. Biblioth Rabbinica, 1, p. 93 (No. 159).

[23] Eichhorn, i., 370. Ersch and Grub. Ency., s. 414.

[24] Qonteres, pref., p 12 and note 5. Ben Bil. belongs to the second
half of the 11th century. See below.

[25] Even Dukes, not the worst of Hebraists says וְאוֹדֶה וְלֹא אֵבוֹשׁ
כִּי אֵיזֶה דְּבָרִים נֶעְלְמוּ מִמֶּנִּי הַהֲבָנָה הַגְּמוּרָה וְלֹא יָדַעְתִּי אִם אֱמֶת אִתִּי
See Qonteres, pref, p 13.

a fact also pointing to the early part of this century.[26] For the earliest grammarians, such as Menahem ben Saruq, wrote in this peculiar kind of rhyme, which took its rise in the time of R, Saadiah Gaon, or a little earlier.[27] (3). The author of these fragments certainly belonged to the land of Palestine, and likely to the school of Tiberias. This appears from his citing *Resh* as one of the letters of double pronunciation (*i.e.* aspirate and soft), a peculiarity of utterance which was heard only in the West.[28] These circumstances make it not improbable that Ben Asher really wrote the fragment in question. Dukes, however, decidedly denies Ben Asher's authorship, and explains the heading of the fragment by supposing that some other writer composed it from reminiscences of Asher's teaching, or perhaps introduced some passages of Asher's actual work into it, and put it forth under the authority of his name. The confusion and perversion that reign in it are so gross that even Hupfeld suspects some false trading under Asher's reputation. As Dukes piously says, יוֹדֵעַ ה׳; meanwhile we may take its own word, and speak of the production as Ben Asher's.

Aharon Ben Asher, then, as he comes before us here, is a poet. And if any conclusion can be drawn from

---

[26] Qonteres, pref , p 10-11, and the citations there Jüd Lit., s. 422 foll.

[27] Dukes, ut sup Menahem flourished about 1000-1020. Beitrage, ii , s 119 Saadiah was *Gaon*, that is, Patriarch of the Babylonian Jews, and died 942. Gesen Gesch., p 96. Dukes, Beitr., ii , p 5 Everything that can be known of this remarkable man and voluminous author has been collected by Dukes in vol. ii of the Beitrage Ewald, in vol. i , has given the substance of much of his comment. on Psalms and Job. As to the use of the poetical measures among the Jews, see Delitzsch, Zur Gesch der Heb. Poesie, s 1-2, 41 fol, 137 folg., Zunz, Synagogale Poesie des Mittelalters, s. 59 folg

[28] Qonteres, pief., p 5, note 4 , and Ben Asher's words, Qonteres, p 38 See the words of Qimchi on this peculiarity of Tiberian enunciation, Buxtorf, Tractatus, p 25

this effort of his muse, he has anticipated that very
popular modern class called metaphysical, that is, he is
mostly unintelligible, dealing in enigmatical similes,
and allusions fetched from infinite distances.   His metre
is not highly polished ; he would have disdained to take
rank among the mechanical rhymers and syllable coun-
ters ; he leaves his lines to expand or contract according
to the expansion or contraction of his ideas.   His verse
may be described, as Hebrew verse best is described, as
"without order or relation ;" the number and character
of his rhymes depending entirely on his humour; which
was variable,   A single stanza will demonstrate his
genius.   After enumerating the accents under several
hard epithets, he closes with the following flourish :—

אֵלוּ הַטְּעָמִים שְׁנִים עָשָׂר

בְּדַעַת וּמוּסָר

מְלֵאִים בְּלִי מַחְסָר

זֶה אִם זֶה נֶאְסָר

כְּמֶלֶךְ וְגִבּוֹר וְשָׂר

The last line is interesting, because it probably gave rise
to the practice long prevalent of classifying the accents
into orders and subordinations like those of an army or
empire.[29]

Ben Asher's tractate contains—I. a treatise on the
prose accents ; and, II., a briefer treatise on the poetical.
The first contains (1), a list of the distinctives, of which
there are twelve (the signs of the Zodiac), and of con-
nectives, of which there are seven (the planets).   Qont.,

---

[29] In Hupf's recension the *King* is amissing.   The usual distinctions
may be seen below, prose table, p, 53.   I. the Emperors; II. the Kings;
III the Princes', the distinctives at the back of the vinculum are all
Officers merely.

pp. 33–36.[30] (2) A pretty extensive section on various matters, the threefold division of Scripture, law, etc., great and small letters, aspirates, gutturals, quiescents, etc., pp. 36–51. (3) A section on Darga and Mercha, the servants of Tbhir, 51–54. (4) A section on Tbhir and its servant Mercha, both on one word (54–55). The second section treats chiefly of the poetic accents. (1) A list of their names, the distinctives being *eight*. These names are very obscure.[31] They are חֹזֵר (Silluq), רִתֵק (Shalsheleth), תִּרֵץ (Dechi), סָלֵק (Olehveyored), נַצַּח (Pazer), תּוֹכֵף (Rbhia), טוֹרֵף (Athnach), גּוֹזֵר (R. Mug.). He gives the name of *Great Shophar* to Legarmeh, which goes along with all the accents, and turns to the East (Mahp. Leg.), or West (Azla Leg.), and is always accompanied by Psiq. And, finally, he names *Muttach*, that is Zinnor, which always accompanies its brother (Oleh.) except four times. And the servants are the *elevated* (Azla), *coming down* (Mercha), *going up* (Munach), *inverted* (Mahpach), *suspended* (Illui), and *between*, that is Tarcha, because, as Baer expounds, it stands always *between* letters, the other Tippecha always coming outside of the letters.[32] (2) After a section, entitled *usage of Azla*, properly belonging to the prose accents, a chapter appears treating of Mercha and Munach and their usage in the beginnings (before Zarqa) and ends of verses (before Silluq). And several passages regarding the place of accent on certain

---

[30] The only peculiar word among the disjunctives is נגדה, which the editor conjectures to be מרעיד (Shalsheleth). The twelfth is Pazer, which is wanting in Hupf.'s recension, who rightly conjectured that it was described under several epithets even in his copy.

[31] Baer gives a *Perush* of these terms. Tor. Em., p. 4–5, note.

[32] These names are all Heb., בין, תולה, פונה, עולה, יורד, מעולה. So are those of the distinctives, a proof of the Western origin of the tract.

words, simple and compound, conclude the recension of
Dukes. That of Hupfeld has many differences.

On account of its extreme confusion, not much re-
liance can be placed on the deductions of this tract. It
has in all probability suffered great hardship and ill-
usage, which has deprived it of its reason. For instance,
it speaks of Rbhia as a servant, and Mercha as a dis-
tinctive; of Shophar (Munach, etc.) as a distinctive,
and Zaqephah—קטנה עֲרוּפָה—an unheard of accent, as
a servant. The relic, however, is venerable.

2. Jehudah Chayyug. Nearest in point of time to
Ben Asher appears the grammarian Jehudah Chayyug.
Chayyug was the first of native grammarians, and wrote
in Arabic. He was a native of Fez in Morocco, where
was a famous Jewish school. Hence he appears with
the title Phasi (פָאסִי) of Fez. His complete name was
Jehuda ben Davud, or Abu-Zacharyah, and also Yachya
(יחיי). It is not impossible that the latter name has
been corrupted by the Berbers into Chayyug.[33] The
exact period of this author's death is not known, though
he probably lived between 1020 and 1040.[34]

Chayyug, besides a dictionary and a work called
Book of Spicery (ס״רקחה)—the former cited by Ben
Gannach, the latter by Aben Ezra[35]—was the author of
three grammatical works, by which his name is best
known. These were composed in Arabic, but soon
found translators into Hebrew, in the persons of Mosheh

[33] Hupf., Commentatio, i., p. 11, note 21. Dukes, Beiträge, ii., p. 155.
Though Chayyug be usually denominated the first of Heb grammarians,
R. Saadia Gaon has the right to that title. Saadyah even wrote a treatise
upon the accents, which is cited by Rashi (Ps xlv. 10) under the name
נקור דר״ סעדיה. Dukes, ii, s. 36 As Rashi did not know Arabic, he
must, if not mistaken, have had before him a Hebrew translation. The
work is otherwise unknown. Dukes, ut sup.
[34] Beiträge, ii, s. 155 Gesen. Gesch., s. 96.
[35] Dukes, ut sup., s. 160, and notes 2, 3.

ben Jeqatilia and Aben Ezra.[36] The original Arabic is to be found in many public libraries, *e.g.* at Oxford; the translations are less common. That edited by Dukes, in his Beiträge, is the translation of Aben Ezra, of which no other copy is known.[37] The first of the three works above mentioned is entitled *Book of Quiescent Letters*, and treats of verbs having a first, second, or third radical a quiescent; the second treats of verbs, double Ayin; and the third tract, called ס'הנקוד, *Book of the punctuation*, is devoted to the vowels and accents.

This tract on the points wants anything like consecutive order or connection. It consists of a number of separate pieces thrown together, and introduced generally by the words שער אחר. The portion of the tract devoted to the accents proper[38] is exceedingly small, and the details very meagre, and not seldom conflicting with the undoubted practice of MSS. Chayyug has not added much to what was delivered by Ben Asher.

Chayyug's list of the accents is very complete, and the names he employs are chiefly those afterwards in use. Peculiar and unexplained, because not occurring elsewhere, is the term *Maqqiph* for Mahpach. The names of the accents are followed by certain mnemonic enigmas, symbolical of the accents, vowels, etc., some of which are not resolvable. A good deal of particular information is given regarding peculiar secutions, illustrated by passages; but the author's rules are not such

---

[36] Jeqatilia, about 1148. Ges as above

[37] Hupf, Comment., i., p 12. Beiträge, p. 158 text and notes.

[38] Technically נקוד refers to the vowels and other diacritic points, טעם to the accents, but they are often used indiscriminately. נגינה refers to the accents as tonic pulsations, the combined musical effect of which is called נעימה. The tract on the punctuation occupies the last and smallest portion of Dukes' vol, pp 179–204. The space given to the accents is small indeed, pp 191–199, and that with interruptions. The editor printed from a MS. in Munich

in general as our present MSS. conform to. He usually introduces his sections with the words ועתה אחל לבאר, and now I will proceed to show. There are several sections so introduced. One consists of an attempt to define when such small words as כי have Metheg and Maqqeph, and when they are independent and have an accent of their own. Another is devoted to a subject not properly accentual, the *labials*; another to the quiescents and aspirates. Then follows one dedicated to Ga'ya, that is Metheg,[39] which is succeeded by another defining the use of two sorts of Munach before Zaq. and Athnach,[40] etc.

All this is succeeded by an important section recapitulating the prose accents and combining with them those of poetry, but proposing a new distribution and nomenclature of both classes, according to their musical values. The three orders into which the author would divide the accents are not very distinct, because his terms are not quite intelligible. The word ידיעה is used to characterise the first class. This word Ben Bilam paraphrases ירום הקול ויעלהו, words which leave the matter somewhat less obscure.[41] Belonging to this class are three prose accents, Pazer, Tlisha, and Geresh; and two poetical, Pazer and Zarqa. The second order is symbolized by the term העמדה, for which Ben Bil. gives מונח.[42] To this class belong, of prose accents, Zaqeph, Yethibh, and Athnach; of poetical, five, Legarmeh, Yethibh, Athnach, Tipp., and Silluq. Under the third term עלוי are arranged the prose accents, Zarqa, Leg.,

---

[39] Not every Metheg is properly Gaya, but only Metheg with Sheva. In reality it is Sheva with Metheg—not Metheg itself—that is Gaya, that is *mugitus*. Luzzatto, Grammatica, p. 37, § 81.

[40] The names are נשואי and קלקל, words referring not to position but music, for both accents stand below.

[41] Beitrage, iii, s. 197, anmerk.   [42] Beitr. ut sup.

Rbh., Tbhir, Tiph, and Silluq, six in number; and one
poetical accent, Rbhia.[43]

It is impossible to form any accurate idea of the rela-
tive tones of the accents from this division. What is
the difference between the first and third class? Both
must consist in high notes. Are the first, perhaps, those
tones that commence low and gradually rise, and the
last those which form a sustained high note? Such a
conjecture might suit several of the accents as distributed
in Chayyug's order, such as Rbhia; but how can Tip-
pecha and Silluq come under the name *Illui* in any
sense? Or, again, how can Zaqeph belong to the second
class, whose note is low and subdued? The prose
accents, at least, seem misplaced in this distribution,
though, perhaps, the classification of the poetical is less
objectionable.

More hopelessly confused still seems the list of poetic
servants, which are said to be Shophar, and Tlisha small
and great! Mahpach and Shophar inferior and Dechuyah
(Dechi), Mercha, Shalsheleth, and Zinnor! The author's
words are in self-contradiction. He tells us there are
eight poetic servants, then he enumerates nine, and adds
"these are *ten* servants to eight accents, in all eighteen."[44]
All this is wound up by some remarks on the accents
that are found repeated. Pazer is said to be repeatable
eight times, 2 Chron. xv. 18.[45] Zarqa and Zaqeph three
times. Several may occur twice, Yethibh (Pashta),
Leg., Tbhir, and Tlisha. The occurrence of two Tlishas
is unique, 2 Sam. xiv. 32.[46]

---

[43] Beitrage, s. 197.
[44] See Hupfeld's attempts to solve the mystery, Commentatio, i., as
above. The passage is indicative of the incorrectness under which the
whole tract labours.
[45] See below, p 54, where *five* is to be corrected eight.
[46] But Michaelis abolishes this solitary passage. See his note, and
Ew., Lehrbuch, s. 174, anmerk 1.

The most interesting part of Chayyug's treatise is the passage which offers the new distribution of the accents musically into three orders. It would be important as well as interesting, were there any reason to consider it correct, and could it be understood. It shows, even as as it stands, that from the first the musical significance of the accents was recognised by the native writers as well as their logical force, and that there does underlie the system this twofold principle of music and logic.

3. Ben Bilam. Third in order among the native writers must be reckoned R. Jehudah Ben Bilam, who belonged to Toledo, and flourished about the end of the 11th and beginning of the 12th century.[47] He is the first who produced a work on the accents, valuable even to our own days. Ben B. seems to have been the author of a number of works. One was a commentary on Isaiah, or some part of it, in which he interprets chap. xi. not of the Messiah but of Hezeqiah. This work has perished.[48] Four compositions, at least, of his are still extant—(1) Book of Verbs, ס" הפעלים, which Polak professes to have copied from a MS. in Leyden,[49] (2) ס" אותית העניינים על מלות, which Polaq interprets as הטעם. (3) ס" התגנים (Tejnis) on ambiguous or synonymous words. (4) ס" טעמי המקרא, his famous work on the accents.

This production contains two parts, one on the prose and another on the poetic accents. They seem both to

---

[47] Dukes, ii., s. 186, anm. 2, zwischen 1080-1100. Polak in 1858 says אשר חי זה שבע מאות ושבעים ש'. Pref., p. 1. Hup., Comment., ii., p. 1. He is cited by Aben Ezra (Ps. iv. 8). Bartolocci, Bib. Rabb., ii, p 188.

[48] Polak, pref, p. 2, mentions a work פירוש על התורה in Arabic, adding אשר מצא החכם שטיינשניידר בעקב ס" אקספורד. Does he mean the work or its *name* merely? See Dukes, s 188, and the quotations given there.

[49] The full title given by Polak is ס" הפ" שנמצאו מנזרות השמות, who adds אשר העתקתי מכ"י מאוצר הס" בליידן. Pref., p. 1.

have been published by Mercier (Mercer), Regius Prof.
of Hebrew at Paris, from the press of R. Stephens; the
poetic in 1556 and the prose in 1565.[50] The work is
found in MS. in a single exemplar. Dukes believed
that only two copies of Mercier's print existed in Ger-
many and Holland, but Hupf, professes to have seen
two in Germany alone.[51] These are only copies of the
portion containing the prose accents; that on the metrical
accents was considered lost by Hup. Recently, how-
ever, a copy has been found in the collection of the
Jewish Society, *Toeleth* (תועלת), in Amsterdam,[52] and
re-edited with a Hebrew pref. and notes by G. J. Polak
of that city, under the title "שער טעמי ג"ס" (1858).
Polak expresses his desire to publish the *three* other
works which he has in his possession.

In this work, Ben Bil. cites a work on the accents,
which he names הוריית הקורא, Direction for the Reader.
Elder writers considered this the work of some other and
unknown author,[53] but later investigators have con-
cluded that the work is by Ben Bilam himself, and also
upon the accents, being nothing else than an earlier
work which he re-cast into the form of his present trea-
tise.[54] A treatise of the same name with that cited by
B. B. is still extant in MS. in Oxford, and a fragment
of it from a transcript by Frausdorf has been published
by Dukes.[55] This MS., though bearing the title "הו' הק"
identical with that of the work which B. B. cites, is not

---

[50] Polak, pref., p. 1, Hupf., Comment., ii., as above.

[51] Dukes, as above, s. 187. Hup., Com. ii., note 2. The copies are in
Marburg and Dresden

[52] As to this Society and its objects *conf* Etheridge, Heb. Lit., p. 395.
Dukes also promises to edit Balam's treatise. Qonteres, pref., p 16

[53] Bartolocci, iii., p 38, sed nomen auctoris ignoratur.

[54] Dukes, ut sup Hup., ut sup, p 7 ff. Indeed B. B. almost expressly
names the work his own when citing it "הק" הו' בספר זכרתי וכבר

[55] Beitrage, ii., s 197, 198, additamente.

itself the same as that work, but identical with the work published by Mercier under the name Taame-ham-Miqra. The MS., moreover, has been translated from the Arabic, which Arabic itself must have been a translation from the Hebrew, which was employed by Balaam.   Further, this MS. contains in it the same citations of the original work, which Mercier's print shows, and altogether, leaving room for necessary deviations arising from transcription and frequent translation, agrees well with our present printed work of Bilaam's.   A small fragment from the MS. has been published by Dukes, p. 198, containing the introduction and the headings of the sections of the poetic part, which, with a few verbal differences, agrees completely with the text reprinted by Polak.

The section of the treatise on the prose accents has been embodied by Heidenheim in his Mishpte-hat-Teāmim, and pretty fully described by Hupfeld.   The chief data of the section on the poetic accents have been incorporated in the following tract with all requisite references.   Any outline of the treatise is thus unnecessary.   Ben Bil., besides being a grammarian, was a hymnologist.   Two *Selichas* are extant said to have been composed by him, one of which is communicated (in a translation) by Zunz.[56]

Many more native writers could be enumerated. R. Jehudah Jequtiel han-Naqdan (הנקדן, the punctuator), wrote עין הקורא, embodied by Heidenheim into his Pentateuch.[57]   R. Shimshon han-Naqdan wrote

---

[56] Commencing בזכרי על משכבי.   Synagogale Poesie, s. 226–7   On the Selicha Literature, see Zunz, s 152, folg. סליחה *penitential* hymn from סלח to *pardon*   Ps cxxx. 4.

[57] Roedelheim, 1818–21   This work was a Masoretic-grammatical production on the Pentateuch and Megilloth.   Jequtiel lived in the middle or

חבור הקונים.[58] Mosheh han-Naqdan was the author of דרכי הנקוד, a work with other titles.[59] Somewhat illustrious is R. Jacob ben-Meir, called *Rabbenu Tam*, the author of a poem on the accents, still extant in MS., commencing אל" לי מגן.[60] He died 1171. The Qimchis (Moses and David, 1190), have left scattered remarks on the accents in their works. A separate treatise by David exists in MS. at Wilna, in the possession of Hirsch Katznelbogen,[61] Others who wrote treatises are R. Meir ben Todros hal-Levi, מסורת סייג לתורה; R. Menachem di Lonzano, אור תורה; R. Menachem ben Shelomoh, of the House of Meir (המאירי), קרית ספר; R. Kalony-mus ben David, שער בטעמים; R. Solomon Nurzi, מנחת שי;[62] Balmesi and many more.

end of 13th century. Heidenheim places him before D. Qimchi. See, on him, Dukes, Qont. pref, p. 17. Steinschneider Handbuch, s. 71. Hupf, Comment., ii, p. 10, and notes. 1250–1300 Jud. Lit.

[58] Delitzsch, Jesurun, s. 16, note, concludes this name to be "ab interpolatore, homine ne med. quidem docto exeogitatum." Shimshon belongs to middle or end of 13th century. Zunz gives 1240, and places his sphere somewhere about the Rhine district. See Delitzsch, Jesurun, s. 16, 241 foll, 257 foll. Hupf., Comment., ii., p. 11, and notes 32, 33, and especially 36, where an outline of his treatise may be found. Dukes, Qont., pref 18.

[59] Printed in the Rabbinic Bibles and several times separately. See Steinsch. Handb., s. 93. Qonteres, s 19. A MS. exists in Munich, containing much more than has been printed (Dukes).

[60] Dukes, Qont., p. 20-21. Hupf. ut sup., p. 10, note 28. Del., Jesurun, s 23. Dukes promises to edit and discuss the song, which consists of 45 verses. Ersch and Grub. Art. Jud Lit., s 417.

[61] היריש קאצנעלבאגען. Dukes, Qont., p. 18. The work is called עט סופר, and mentioned both by Lonzano and Nurzi.

[62] On all the above, see Dukes, pref to Qonteres Hammasoreth Steinschneider Handbuch. Etheridge, Heb. Lit. On Nurzi, also see the Introductions. Ersch and Gruber Encyclop. Art. Jud Literatur. Also the English Jewish Literature by Steinschneider, Longman, 1857. Bartolocci Biblioth. Rabbinica. Fürst Biblioth. Judaica. Luzzatto Prolegomem, etc. etc.

HEBREW ACCENTUATION.

§ 1. ACCENT. USES.

"Accent means the following things. (1) It means the pitch of the voice, as high or low, acute or grave, the tune or tone of articulated speech; and this it means in a triple application. *First*, it has this meaning with respect to the syllables of a word, the syllabic accent. *Second*, it has this meaning with respect to the word or words of a sentence, the clause of an oratorical period. One clause of a period we say is spoken in a high key, another in a low. *Thirdly*, it has this meaning partly at least in respect to the character of national or provincial enunciation. (2) Accent means superior stress or energy of vocal utterance, given to certain syllables of a word or words of a sentence, in comparison of those with which they are connected. In the case of syllables, the accent is specially called syllabic; in the case of sentences, it corresponds with what is perhaps more commonly called the oratorical emphasis. (3) Accent with modern writers on music is employed to denote that prominence which, by means of a more marked tonic impulse, is given by a singer or player to one note of a series of notes called a bar, above the other notes of the bar"[1]

[1] Blackie. Rhythmical Declamation of the Ancients, p. 1 f.

These few sentences, abridged from a writer thoroughly acquainted with the subject, exhaust the common significations of accent. The third signification or meaning in music we are not at present specially concerned with; the musical accent, if regarded at all in prose declamation, must be considered coincident with rhetorical accent. The synagogal delivery is a kind of song, but this song is founded on, and but a degeneration of proper oratorical delivery. Neither are we here concerned with provincial accent, with the tone or twang of one district as differing from the twang of another. Different families of Jews do cantillate the same accents by different melodies, but this is not to be explained on the principle of provincial pronunciation. Of the significations therefore noticed by Professor Blackie we shall need to attend only to the first and second. Hebrew accents exhibit *pitch* of key, *stress* of utterance, and each of these perhaps in a threefold way; pitch and stress of the syllable in a word, pitch and stress of the word in a clause, pitch and stress of the clause in a verse.

Hebrew accents have formally another use different from any of the uses served by accents in non-Semitic languages: they are signs of logical interpunction. This use as a rule is coincident with their use as symbols of stress and pitch, because it is the logical relations of the various members of a verse which rule the pauses and modulations of the voice in declaiming that verse. The Hebrew accents are the complement of the Hebrew vowels. They bear the same relation to the *verse* that the vowels do to the *word*. Both are a species of phonography, the vowel signs representing all the vowel sounds and shades of sound evolved in every individual word in speech; the accents representing all the pauses and connections, elevations and depressions, attenuations and intensifications of voice, occurring in reading the Bible as a piece of composition in religious service.

1. The accents mark the tone-syllable of each word.

This duty all accents perform alike. Obviously, how-ever, this cannot be the exclusive function of the accents, for a single symbol would have been for this purpose sufficient.

2. The accents are signs of logical interpunction like our points.[2] They are in this sense only relative, not like our points absolute, that is, they divide a verse into members relatively to each other and the whole verse: but it is not necessary that these members or even the whole verse should contain complete and independent meaning, like our period. It may take several Hebrew verses or Pasuqim to form a complete logical period, and on the other hand a single Pasuq may contain several complete logical periods. This logical use, and the use as indicators of the tone-syllable, are important, and deserving of some attention from Biblical scholars. The accents will be found of great advantage as keys to syntax and grammar.[3] But it is obvious that these two uses do not exhaust the purposes served by the accents. It not unfrequently happens that we find them placed on the syllable of a word which we know not to be in ordi-nary circumstances the tone-syllable,[4] and they frequently

---

[2] In this use the accents are named טְעָמִים *senses*, marks of sense, that is, signs of logical interpunction.

[3] See what Ewald says of the connection of accent and syntax in the Anhang to his Grammar on that subject, p 752 ff.

[4] And hence some scholars have denied entirely their use as indicators of the place of tone So Saalschütz, Form der Hebräischen Poesie, ed. Hahn, p 197 ff There is no doubt that this writer is here in error (1) The place of accent is known in ordinary circumstances, such as inflections, declension, etc, not so much from actually observing the position of the accentual symbol as from the vowel changes and trans-formations which we know to be occasioned by its change of place. The whole vowel system of the Masoretes is essentially connected with a pronunciation of the language as at present accented. Their accentuation may be wrong, just as their vowel system may be, but their accentuation and vowel system go together; and they certainly meant in ordinary cir-cumstances to put their accentual signs on the syllable of the word which bears the tone. (2) In the Assyrian accentual system, which is closely allied to the common Masoretic, as exhibited in the Odessa MS, the accents always stand on the tone-syllable, and do not present the deviations in position shown by the common system See Ewald, Iahrbücher, 1848.

enter into combinations which are inconsistent with logic
and syntax For example, certain great distinctives
must have certain smaller distinctives before them,
though syntax and logic should demand a connective
instead of a distinctive, and many words, even mono-
syllables (Gen. v., 29) appear with two accents or some-
times as many as three (Job. vi., 10) a phenomenon
which can have no reference to logic.

3. These peculiarities are explained by the third prin-
ciple governing the use of the accents; they are rhyth-
mical signs. that is, representations of the modulations
and inflections of the living voice in declamation or
cantillation.[5] In the service of the synagogue this is
the chief purpose the accentuation serves. There is a
kind of melody,[6] halfway between oratory and song,
chaunted in reading, and there is no doubt that the
accentual signs serve for this melody the purpose of
musical notes. At the same time, the same accents are
said to be susceptible of being cantillated in different
ways, the Polish Jews observing one method, the Spanish
Jews another and simpler method; and, what is more
remarkable still, the same passage is cantillated on
different occasions, such as the Passover, with a melody

---

[5] In this sense, that is, as *modi*, or symbols of modulation, the accents
are called נגינות, נְגִינָה properly κρουμός (Hupf.) just as in the Talmud
זִמְרָה is employed of the modulations of the voice in public reading.
Until the investigations of modern scholarship brought to light the logical
principle of the accentuation and thus set it on its true basis—a combined
logico-rhythmical—the Jews considered it to be exclusively musical. It
is in their estimation a remnant, altogether confused and misunderstood,
of the ancient temple music, the restoration of which shall accompany the
restoration of the nation under the Messiah See Hupfeld Ausfuhr.
Heb. Gramm p 116, etc, Gesenius Geschichte der Heb Sprache, p.
219 ff

[6] *Reading* is a peculiarity of Europeans All Orientals sing and accom-
pany themselves with demonstrative signs and gesticulations The Arabs
chant their Qor'an; all half barbarian nations use a chant in their service,
just as in the early church the Scriptures were chanted, and even among
ourselves, no later than the last century and the beginning of this, a kind
of song was employed in reading the Scriptures, even in Presbyterian
Churches

different from that of the usual Sabbath day cantillation.

Does, then, the accentuation embody a music? Here we are on the brink of a Serbonian bog, where armies whole of disputants have sunk. What do we mean by music? Music and cantillation are different things, although at times cantillation rises nearly to music, as at other times music, especially ancient music, sinks almost to cantillation. The Hebrews, however, had a magnificent music; it was almost the only liberal art in which they excelled. It would be almost absurd to imagine that the grand melodies of the Temple never rose above the hum-drum of the modern synagogue. Writers, indeed, on music, have been so misled as to assert that in the ancient music there were no bars, or what is the same thing, time. Music is impossible without time or accent; whether bars as signs of accent were invented by the ancients or not, is of small enough moment. But dancing implies the recognition of musical accent, and the universal employment of cymbals, which were used to beat time and give the sign for certain movements, is demonstrative of the same thing. In the grand and solemn, as well as triumphal music of the ancient Temple, there was doubtless everything present which is present in our own music. Whether it possessed a notation or not, or if it did, under what form, we cannot discover. The present accentual signs, or some of them, may have served for such notes, and may be a kind of reminiscence of them, although the fact that different schools, such as the Tiberian and the Assyrian, invented or employed different symbols, seems to prove the reverse, and bring down the rise of the present signs to a very much later period. The question is itself not very important; it is enough to know that this Temple music is, according to the Jews' own confession, now lost; it may be an echo of it, confused and broken, which we have in the accents, but itself it is not. Floating fragments of it, which have been caught up by ear after ear, and preserved religiously through exile and dispersion, may be still found in the melodies chanted in the synagogues, but this we cannot affirm; what we know is, that even the poetic accentuation lays no claim to represent this music in anything like completeness.

Another and very different thing from the real Temple music, was the solemn delivery of the Scriptures in the synagogues. The institution of the synagogue dates after the exile; after, therefore, the great leaders of the Temple music, the Asaphs and sons of Korah, were no more, and when that music itself was either lost or falling into confusion, and its meaning misunderstood. This reading of the Scriptures was, like all Oriental reading, a kind of song. Between the prose and poetic books some distinction was doubtless observed, inasmuch as the latter were more regular, more rhythmical, and more susceptible of real musical utterance. This solemn style of delivery was preserved by tradition, handed down almost as a part of the sacred Scripture itself, the tones of the ancestral voice were hallowed, the venerable accents in which the Word had been read from time immemorial were holy; a reverent posterity would not willingly let them die; they recalled, and ever onward and forward perpetuated the living voices of holy men and prophets, many of whom had held communion with God himself. And thus arose the accentual system, and this is its meaning. It is not and cannot be any remnant of the Temple music, for, with reference to prose, that is ridiculous; and all fundamental investigation demonstrates the priority of the prose accents, and indicates that these were used as the norm and standard for those of poetry. It is simply the synagogal delivery, the traditional living utterance of the reader, seized and photographed, and handed down to us as a precious monument of ancient pulpit oratory. It is possible that these public readers and expounders may have preserved in the poetic books some fragments of the former melodies of the Temple; their ears may have caught up

strains which their memories still retained across the
long captivity, and these might still, as familiar sounds,
ever and naturally find expression in their reading, and
the declamation thus pass over into perfect music. That
something of this kind is not unlikely, is evident from
the very peculiar accentuation of some of the Psalms,
which are very different in many respects from the other
poetic books, Job and Proverbs, in the fine play of the
smaller accents, and the frequent employment of double
or even triple accents on the same word; but a complete
music, or a music exclusively, we have not even here.

It is marvellous, if these accents are really notes of an
actual melody, how they are susceptible of being cantil-
lated in different ways. The Polish Jews observed one
method, and the Spanish Jews another and simpler
method. The Germans accuse the Spaniards and the
Italians of not paying sufficient attention to the smaller
distinctives and servants, and of singing the greater dis-
tinctives only; while the Spaniards, on the other hand,
accuse the German method of obscurity and confusion.[7]
And we should doubtless wrong them both if we thought
their charges ill-founded.

Then another peculiarity is observable. On different
occasions, such as the Passover, the same passage of
Scripture, accented in the same way, is sung with a
melody widely different from that which accompanies it
on ordinary occasions. And different books, though
accented precisely in a similar way, are very differently
cantillated. The books of Moses are chanted, they tell
us, in a tone full and sweet; the prophecies in accents
rude and pathetic; the Psalms of David with an air
grave and partaking of ecstasy; the Proverbs of Solomon
in an insinuating manner; the Song with joy and mirth;
Ecclesiastes in a tone serious and severe:[8] it is even
forbidden to the musician to change the tone, under pain

---

[7] Jablonski, Pref. in Bib. Heb, 24, note r.
[8] Saalschütz, Form der Heb Poesie, p. 184, note.

of excommunication. And yet all these different books, on'
which so many different tones are expended, are marked,
with the exception of the Psalms, with the same accents.
The observation of this fact has operated naturally in two
different ways :

1. It has compelled some to deny altogether the
musical use of the accents. Mr. Cross proclaims him-
self among this number :—" It is not unworthy observa-
tion what *Bohlius* says, that the Jews (*falsely*, and not
without Satan's cunning) say the use of the *accents* is
musical, an art only known to the Jews, etc. If the
accents give laws to the sacred verse, then the songs of
praise and most bitter lamentations are sung both with
one tune ; an intolerable absurdity. Compare Job, iii. 3,
with Ps. lxvi., and Job, iii. 8, with Ps. lxvi. 8, the
points are the same—David's jubilee and triumphal
songs sung to the tune of *cursed be the day*."[9]

2. Others have endeavoured to reconcile these pecu-
liarities with the theory that the accents in their present
form are proper musical composition. The disagreement,
it is said, between the Polish and Spanish Jews is chiefly
in appearance ; the latter use a plainer and simpler
style, the former intercalate more grace notes ; but the
difference consists perhaps in nothing more fundamental.
Still this reduces the precision of the so-called notation
considerably ; it can only, being capable of such diverse
treatment, represent the outlines of a melody. But
further, seeing the accent or note attaches itself to one

---

[9] Taghmical Art, p 14. Mr. C. has many arguments on this head.
" Add further that it is scarcely credible they should sing the name of the
musical instrument, the musician in chief, with the occasion and preface ;
but yet all these in Scripture bear the same points with the song." "No
lyrick licence in Horatian or Pindaric odes will comprehend the Psalms of
David. No comical dimensions used in Terentius or Plautus can confine
any Hebrew verse except by accident" Again, "Gomarus in his *Lyra*
has this rule (reg 5), 'The Hebrew verse are first, various, secondly, of
various feet; thirdly, more or mixed, fourthly, short or long; fifthly,
analogous or anomalous; sixthly, excessive or defective, seventhly, of
many kinds, without order or relation' It had been sooner said—any
prose makes Hebrew verse," p 16.

syllable only, and many syllables may intervene be-
tween the notes, it appears at once that each accent
cannot be simply a single note ; it must be several : in
short, the accents represent each a musical *phrase*. This
is a fundamental position of all who maintain the pre-
sence of complete music in the accents. On this hypo-
thesis the Jewish *Zarqas*,[10] or scales, are formed. Each
accent is itself a little song, a complete expression.
Whenever, therefore, this accent presents itself, the cor-
responding phrase should be chanted, but this will not
be found to be the case in modern cantillation. Still,
one, and the chief difficulty, lies in the way. How shall
we account for totally *different* melodies being chanted
in different countries, and on different occasions, to the
same accents ? So far, it will be answered, as these
melodies differ only in rapidity of march, there can be
no difficulty. The same notes may be chanted slow or
quick, and are capable of being resolved into any notes
equivalent in time, though much superior in number, to
the normal notes. And secondly, so far as the notes of
the various melodies differ in pitch or relation, it must
be maintained that the present accentuation gives a
musical *fundamental*.[11] It is sufficient to put readers
upon the track of the question, without ourselves pur-
suing it ; for all intended by this tract will be accom-
plished, if the attention of Hebrew students be directed

[10] So called from the first note, *Zarqa*. Such a scale, though very
incorrect, may be seen in Jablonsky, Heb. Bible, vol. i. § 24. The
same, corrected, Saalschutz, Form der Heb. Poesie, appendix.

[11] Any one wishing to see more on this subject may consult Paulus, Neues
Repertorium für Bib und Morgenland Literatur, Theil I.-III., Jena,
1790-91, where a writer of the name of Anton gives a detailed scheme of
music from the accents. According to this writer the prose accents present
the melody, the poetic accents the bass, and hence at the same time the
whole harmony, since the Oriental music consisted simply of concords.
The position of an accent above or below the line is of much consequence;
standing above, its tone is to be pitched an octave higher than if it stands
under. Saalschütz gives a very fair, but unfavourable criticism, on Anton's
labours, Form der Heb. Poesie, Anhang ub die Musik d. Hebräer,
p 370

to the difficulties and the problems involved in the accentual system. This whole subject of the accentual music is especially obscure. The relation of those accents called servants or connectives to their disjunctives, and of disjunctives to each other, appears inexplicable, if each has a proper musical value; and equally inexplicable is their variety and number, if each has not a proper value. The relation between the servants and their masters is such, that if the servant be present there will be harmony, if it be absent there will be harmony; if another in many cases accept its functions and stand in its place, there will be harmony. And equally flexible and conciliatory are the disjunctives. A fundamental setting at rest of the question is, now, with our meagre and contradictory information on Hebrew music and declamation, not to be looked for. Thus much we may safely say, the principle of the accentuation is twofold, musical and logical; not first musical and then subordinately logical, nor yet first logical and subordinately musical; but primarily and fundamentally musicological, the one undivided expression of the two factors fused and melted into homogeneous unity. It is photographed, phonographed oratory. And so far as different families of Jews, or the same family on different occasions, intone the same piece of accented Scripture in different ways, and pretend that both or all the different ways are legitimate renderings of the same accents, they speak what is incredible and even absurd, and only prove their own ignorance and incapacity.[12]

Radically the same problem under another name has

[12] Without knowing the values of the different accents—for of course in the *system* they have values, although they cannot be gathered from the present Jews—any attempt to cantillate must be only abortive and ludicrous. Mr Cross well says, " But I think they have more time than wit to spare that can bestow much of it in learning or teaching that art " P. 15. It is almost trifling to speak of an authoritative cantillation, but the Rabbins frequently appeal to the logical force of the accents as authoritative in *hermeneutics*. See the well-known words of Abenezra, Buxtorf, p 256

to be discussed under the question, does the Hebrew accentuation embody a *rhythmus?* Are the accents rhythmical? Here. again, we have two questions not identical. We answer the first negatively, the second affirmatively. The Hebrew accentuation embodies no rhythmus, but for all that it is rhythmical. Its tendency is towards a rhythmus What is a rhythmus? We call any regular recurrence of *sounds* a rhythmus; it is the expression of a law, by which the same series of sounds ever present themselves anew. A trochee is a combination of sounds, a long and short, or accented and unaccented; any composition where this foot regularly occurs is a rhythmus. The rhythmus will not be destroyed by the occasional admission of other sounds, provided these have such a relation to the trochees that the latter still predominate and throw their influence and character over the whole. In this sense Hebrew accentuation forms no rhythmus. It has, doubtless, trochees, and jambi, and spondees, but nothing like regular combination of them.[13] In all speech such feet occur, whether Hebrew or other speech But Hebrew accentuation technically is not a syllable accentuation at all; it is a word accentuation, and its rhythmus therefore, if one exist, must be a word rhythmus.

This principle has been seized and experimented on with the design of extracting the elements of a rhythmus from it by various scholars. It is conceivable that in delivery a man might accent every second word strongly (*i.e.* utter strongly the tone-syllable), leaving the intermediate word, though with its tone-syllable of necessity

---

[13] It is true that Josephus, Jerome, etc., call the Hebrew measure *hexameter*, but it would puzzle a modern scholar to lay his hand on many such lines. An occasional hexameter may occur by accident, just as in the English version of Ps. 2, the first line is a pure hexameter Why do the | heathen | rage and the | people im | agine a | vain thing? or as James fell into a hexameter in the passage πᾶσα δόσις, etc It was a desire to emulate the Greek and Latin poetry that revealed to the ancients Greek and Latin feet in Hebrew.

marked, yet with much less appreciable emphasis; or that
on every second word the reader elevated his voice and on
the intermediate word depressed it, making such a flow as
this ‿́‿‿́‿‿ etc. · it is further conceivable that the
emphasised notes, besides standing in a certain relation
of strength or elevation to the intermediate and un-
emphasised, might stand in a graduated relation to each
other; one might possess an emphasis double or triple
that of the other, or it might be half or one-third the
height or pitch of the other, furnishing such a flow
as the following : read from the right.

etc. ‿‿″‿‿́

Once more, such a rhythmus, for both the last and the
former are actually rhythmi, may be a duplicate or a
triplicate, that is, may occur in pairs or in sets of three

etc. |″‿‿́|‿″‿″‿́|‿″‿″‿́   (a)

or |″‿″‿́|‿‴‿″‿́|‿‴″‿‿́ · (b)

Something like the Dichotomy (a) has been the gene-
rally received fundamental of the rhythmus, and is still
insisted upon by most Hebraists who have attended to
the question, e.g. Hupfeld. The Trichotomy (b) has
been taken under the patronage of Ewald, who is its
inventor and strenuous defender. Not, however, in its
naked simplicity, as given above. It is further con-
ceivable that even the weakly accented words or *sinkings*
(in contradistinction to the strongly emphasised words
or *elevations*) may bear to each other a relation similar
to that in which the distinctives stand to each other;
these also may form a succession of regularly increasing
or decreasing sounds, increasing from the beginning of
the verse in heaviness, decreasing in the same propor-
tion and direction in pitch. And, finally, it may be
that this triple principle runs through all the system,
the typal form of every division great or small, the
inner skeleton being ever a triad of pulsations. One
great *Dreiklang* developes itself in the whole extent of

the verse, breaking it up into three divisions, stepping like a giant in three vast strides from end to end, every step increasing in the heaviness of its tread; under its legs numberless others peep about to find themselves places, till the whole Pasuq is measured out into three, and each of these three again into three, and these subdivisions again multiplied by three, until the whole is complete and harmonious. The voice, starting at the commencement of a Pasuq, utters its first word high but thin, it goes on decreasing in the height of its pitch, but increasing in the heaviness of its emphasis, through successive jolts, till it passes segolta, athnach (or merchamahpach and athnach in poetry), and finally lowest but heaviest, resposes in silluq; but in its passage numberless triads have formed themselves into individuality. The accentual principle is a crystal, which, fracture it how you may, and be its fragments great or small, breaks ever into threes.

Any conclusion which this grammarian comes to demands the most respectful attention. No man has thought more profoundly on Hebrew Grammar, and, with the exception of Hupfeld, he is the only man in the present century who has made an independent philosophical study of the accents; and those who will take the trouble to read his treatise on the subject, Lehrbuch, p. 160—218, will acknowledge that he has done more than any man living to discover the *rationale* of many of the accentual combinations.

The grand objection, however, to this theory, as to all others—apart from the objections of excessive complexity and subtle ingenuity, which apply to it specially—is that it is inconsistent with facts. The Trichotomy is non-apparent. Open any verse in the Hebrew Bible, and ten to one not a threefold but a twofold division meets us; analyse any of the minor divisions of the verse and we perceive the same thing. It is impossible to divide the accents of one verse out of a hundred into sets of three, or into sets of any definite number of

pulses. Combinations of all sorts appear, twos, threes,
and all heaped irregularly together. The author himself
acknowledges that in the even flow of the last verse-row
(Silluq's clause), after the first trilogy[14] has expended
itself, and when we are looking for another, this second
is not forthcoming; it is only rudimentary, consisting
of a single pulsation, coupled with two depressions.
This is its common appearance; but into what a long
sweep it may expand itself he himself has shown, where
we hear no more of triple pulsation, but the accents
press thick and close upon one another. It may be said
that the triple pulsation will appear when possible. But
this is giving up the theory. To be sure there are im-
perfect lines in Virgil, but what should we say of
hexameters which consisted sometimes of six, sometimes
of four, or five, or two or three feet, and these, whenever
they extended beyond two, only accidentally the same
kind of feet? There seems indeed to be no complete
rhythmus exhibited by the accents. There may be a
tendency towards rhythmical expression,[15] there may be
fragments of rhythm, just as there are fragments of
music in the cantillation, but the tendency has never
reached perfect realization. It even remains a question
what the base was, if any, towards which there was a
striving. The older accentuists, who held faster to the
logical than the rhythmical principle, though not alto-
gether denying the latter, were unanimous in concluding
the rhythmus to be a dichotomy, or antithesis, a pro-
gressive evolution into pairs. These pairs were con-
sidered homogeneous by Spitzner,[16] who has most fully
unfolded this theory; that is, pairs of periods, pairs of
propositions, pairs of concepts, in general pairs of similar

[14] Ewald's fundamental trilogy consists of the first line of our prose
table, § 5

[15] Compare Delitzsch's Introduction to his Commentary on the Psalms,
and his translations of the various psalms

[16] See Spitzner's Institutiones, chap iii, De Dichotomia, and the
whole concluding portion of the work Hupf in der Zeits der D. M.
Gesellschaft, 6ter Band, s 153 ff.

members. This is a rhythm produced by the balance of thought and expression, which gave rise also to balance of tone and impulse. There is often a tendency to use the word rhythmus in an obscure way. Ewald, for instance,[17] and many others, talk of a *sense rhythmus,* an expression to which there seems attached or attachable no exact idea. The judge of a rhythmus is the ear. A rhythmus consists of sounds or regular succession of sounds. These sounds may be articulate or inarticulate. Obviously the meaning of the sounds cannot form any element in the rhythmus, or we might speak quite as logically of a *colour* rhythmus. The regular recurrence of *ideas,* as expressed in popular refrains, cannot with any meaning be called a rhythmus, unless expressed in regular laws of sound. Neither can Hebrew poetry be said to embody a rhythmus merely because it exhibits parallel ideas, or regular recurrence or intensification of the same idea. Unless these be expressed in sounds succeeding each other by a certain law, there cannot properly be any rhythmus.

The Hebrew accentuation cannot therefore strictly embody a real rhythmus. There may be a law, but the law is not strictly observed; or like the music in cantillation, there may be fragments of various kinds of rhythmus, but no single principle carried out fully and exclusively. Still the system is rhythmical and not simply logical. Our modern interpunction is barely logical according to meaning. It is interpunction of written sense, not uttered or declaimed sense. Hebrew punctuation is punctuation of the living utterance. And as speech, especially oratory, when natural, is musical or rhythmical, so the Hebrew accents, being the interpunction of oratory, will themselves be rhythmical. The voice coming through the channel of the organs of

---

[17] Dichter des Alten Bundes, i. p 57ff. A marvellously clear sketch of ancient and modern opinions on this subject may be seen in De Wette's Introduction to his Commentary on the Psalms, 5te Auflage, s 32 folg

utterance, resembles a tide running through a strait.
It may be high or low, variable or equable, strong or
feeble, slow or rapid. In point of fact, several or all of
these varieties will be contained in a single verse, or
section of the stream of speech. Words, like masses of
water rolling inland, rise and fall, swell and sink, oscillate
and impinge on each other, and dash with strong im-
pulse on every obstacle, gradually increasing in might
as they approach the shore, where they break in greatest
force and die away in silence. These obstacles, where
the wave is seen to rise and curl, might be compared to
the greater pauses or elevations of the voice, marked
in composition with the chief distinctive accents, the
equable roll to the clause of words under the power of
this accent, where the voice remains much at one pitch,
and the final dash to the concluding pause, where
the energy of the voice is greatest though the pitch be
lowest. Hebrew accentuation undertakes to represent
by a system of symbols this almost infinite variety of
modulation of voice. The accentual system must there-
fore be almost endlessly complex. No inflection, no
pause, no intensification of voice, but is presented to the
eye. Before the application of external symbols, a
peculiar declamation had become traditional. Even this
mode of public reading was considered sacred, and lest
the unskilled should innovate and so profane the Scrip-
tures, a system of signs was invented which should stereo-
type the delivery for all time coming. We may take
for granted that even in Hebrew accentuation, compli-
cated and childish as it looks, there will be found nothing
arbitrary. It is the expression of logic and music com-
bined, or it might be said to be oratorical delivery so
much exaggerated in its inflections and pauses as to
stand nearly allied to music ; and though it is most
unprofitable to seek to imitate the cantillation of the
synagogue, a rational exegesis will have no better guide
than the accents considered as logical signs ; and even
considered as signs of modulation, a good reader of

Hebrew, who delivers according to our western mode of reading, if he possess the usual amount of inflections in his voice, will almost absorb the whole system of the prose accentuation, and give to each accent, if not the exact sounds in the exact degree given them by the Jewish reader, yet relatively the same sounds, and relatively in the same degree, as even the Jew gave them.[18]

[18] Whoever wishes full information regarding attempts to restore the rhythm of the poetic accents, or of the poetry without the accents, that is either according to or against the Masoretic verse, may consult De Wette's Einleitung to his Com on the Psalms, and the books there referred to. An interesting attempt to restore the strophical form of a whole book is exhibited by Schlottmann, Das Buch Hiob verdeutscht, u erlautert, Berlin, 1850, though the attempt is pronounced a failure by the author of a masterly review reprinted in the British and Foreign Evang. Review for July, 1857 On the subject of *parallelism*, may be consulted Lowth, Lectures on Heb Poetry; Fairbairn, Hermeneutical Manual, p. 166, etc.; Forbes, Scripture Parallelism, Ewald, Dichter d Alt Bundes I, s 57 ff and s 92 ff.; also Koster, Strophen od. Parallelismus der heb. Poesie, Stud u Krit, 1831, erster Theil, s 40 folg.

§ 2. ANTIQUITY AND AUTHORITY.

The supposed authority of the accents is very de-
pendent on their supposed antiquity. The accents form
now a part of all our printed Bibles. The fact is cu-
rious. Why are they there, and by what authority?
Here on the one hand we are in danger of falling under
the influence of a derationalizing superstition, and on
the other, under the guidance of a supercilious flippancy,
the well-beloved child of ignorance. The early reformed
theologians looked on the accents as a divine institution,
the immediate handiwork of Moses or Ezra, men com-
missioned of God, among other things, to bequeath this
precious legacy to coming generations. The present
race of men, conceited and ungrateful, look upon what
Buxtorf reverenced as an effort of uncreated Wisdom,
with contempt, as the childish finicalities of "mecha-
nical" Jews. It is probable that the first opinion and
the last are equally impertinent. We should hardly *à
priori* expect an accentual revelation; and, lest *à priori*
disproof should not carry conviction, it is enough to say
that no evidence of such revelation is forthcoming.
There are rabbinic testimonies enough, but so there are
to many things that are impossible. At the same time
we set out from the principle that a deliberately con-
ceived and intricately worked out system, such as the
Hebrew accentuation, must have a purpose and a mean-
ing; and that Jews, though at times harbouring foolish
conceits, are much on a level as to rationality with other
creatures. Hence we expect to find an *intention* at least
in the accentuation, whether fully realised or not. And
as all Jewish intentions looked in one direction, that of
preserving inviolate their divinely inspired Scriptures.
it is probable that if we can really read the intention of

the accents, we shall not have lost, but gained in our esteem for human reverence and religious care, as well as in our accurate understanding of the Bible.

The system of accents, then, is neither to be attributed to highest divine wisdom nor deepest human folly. It is the result of a peculiar critical development of the human mind, a development not unconnected with other similar tendencies which appeared simultaneously, or in close succession, in Arabia on the south, and in Syria on the north of Palestine. We would be wrong in limiting this critical bent to any single family of the Semitic race, or circumscribing its activity to a very narrow circle of years. The three chief families of Semites seem to have manifested the tendency in common, priority to some degree in point of time and influence being due to the Syrians, who in their turn were stimulated by their contact and rivalry with the Greeks, and by the new mental energy communicated by the reception of the Christian religion and its sacred literature. We would be wrong in venturing to say that this peculiar criticism arose in such a year and expired in such another. Minds are exceedingly slow of motion. A direction cannot be communicated to a national mind without the concurrence of many forces, the application and success of which requires many years. And as mental springs are only gradually and painfully bent, they are only gradually and with difficulty relaxed. A critical tendency will not terminate so abruptly that a precise date can be assigned to its expiry. If we take the close of the Talmud[1] on the one side and the close of the tenth century on the other, embracing a period of four or five hundred years, we shall have room enough for that peculiar class of men who conceived and completed the so-called Masoretic vowel and accentual system. Neither

---

[1] The Talmudic period was of about 310 years duration—188 to 498. Keil, Einleitung, s. 596 Leop Dukes, Sprache der Mischnah, s 15 Authorities do not entirely agree. Conf Zunz, Die gottesdienstlichen Vortrage der Juden, historisch entwickelt, s. 52 ff.

the vowels nor the accents are the discovery of one individual—they are likely the slow growth of centuries.
Acute critics have noticed in different books of the Bible
a slight difference of vocalization.[2] So, too, in the
Hagiographa, a somewhat different accentuation is observable from that current in the other books, *e.g.*, in
the frequent use of the accents Pazer and Qarnepharah,[3]
showing unmistakeably a difference of hands.

Regarding antiquity and authority, a rational criticism
cannot entertain any doubts on these two points—*first*,
the novelty of the present vocalic and accentual *signs ;*
second, the antiquity of the sounds and style of declamation which they signify ; the twofold accuracy with
which tradition has handed down the pronunciation of
the Bible text, and with which the present system of
Masoretic points represents it. The briefest outline only
of argument can be offered in support of these positions.[4]

(*a*) The peculiar nature of the Semitic word-stem.

---

[2] Ewald, Lehrbuch, p 136

[3] Ibid , p. 207, 99*a*. See, on the gradual rise and nature of the perfectly similar Syriac punctual system, Ewald, Abhandlungen zur Orient.
u Bib. Literatur, Erster Theil, art in p. 63 foll

[4] The first to fight the current Jewish dogma of the divinity of the
points, and their Mosaic, or at least Ezraitic origin, was Elias Levita,
himself a Jew. The modern invention of the accents and vowel signs has
been most ably maintained by Ludovicus Cappellus, Arcanum punctationis revelatum, published first by Erpenius, 1624. The other side has
been supported with great learning by the younger Buxtorf, in reply to
Cappellus, in his Tractatus de punct. origine, antiquitate, etc , 1648 ; a
work containing much information on other subjects besides those in
immediate dispute. The reader may consult, in addition to the above
fundamental works (Spitzner, Vindiciæ originis et auctor divinæ punct
vocal, Lips, 1791, said to contain full information on the stages of the
controversy and the circumstances of the disputants), Carpzov. Critica
Sacra, chap v s. 7, in favour of the divine authority ; Brian Walton's
proleg to his Polyglot, in 38 foll against it, also Keil, Einleitung,
s. 510 foll , Davidson's Bib. Criticism, p 37 foll. In the present century the subject has been again most thoroughly discussed by Hupfeld,
Beleuchtung dunkler Stellen der Alttest. Textgeschichte, Studien u
Kritiken, 1830, p 549, etc , and 1837, p 830 foll , which may be
regarded as demonstrative of the post-Talmudic origin of the present
punctual *symbols* Also coinciding generally with Hupfeld, Ewald, Lehrbuch, p. 121 142

The idea lay in the bare consonantal stem itself; the modification of idea lay in the modified stem. But as the modification was either a change of vowel inside or a very apparent addition outside, the triliteral stem was itself still recognisable, and the fundamental idea it conveyed immediately suggested. Even the peculiar modification of idea was often suggested by a prefixed or added consonant, which was also a sort of index what vowel change was at the same time introduced, and altogether with the surrounding sense left a reader who was well versed in the tongue at no loss for the exact pronunciation and meaning.

To this has to be added the analogy of the other languages. In general the Semitic tongues are not vocalized. The Qor'an,[5] it is true, was vocalized soon after Mohammed's death, but other works usually present the bare consonantal text. The Syrians most probably communicated the idea of a complete vocalization to the Jews, having themselves borrowed it from the Greeks. The Jewish Grammarians, however, far outstripped their Syrian guides and forerunners.

(b) The peculiar aspect of the present Masoretic text. Very early the Jews employed the consonants ו and י to express certain vowel or diphthongal sounds, especially when final; they also employed א and ה, particularly the latter, for the same purpose. And the Greek alphabet shows that this tendency appeared in very early times, and included even *ayin* among the vowel representatives. At first these vowel letters or *matres lectiones* were used very sparingly and only under necessity, and seldom are to be seen in the earlier books except where they are final or where there is a concourse of vowels; but in later Hebrew, when the Aramean began to intrude upon the Palestinian speech, and the native language was less perfectly understood, writers such as Jeremiah and Ezechiel find it necessary to give the *scriptio plena*, that is, to vocalize much more frequently; and not

---

[5] Theodor Noldeke, Geschichte des Qorâns, s. 305 folg. Goettingen, 1860.

seldom this vocalization of theirs conflicts with the
Masoretic system afterwards superinduced upon it, *e.g.*
כולם for כֻּלָּם‎, הובנים for הַבֹּ‎ "(höb).

And to this attaches itself the whole question of the
Qri and Kthibh, the latter being the consonantal text
which the vocalizer worked upon, and in which, from
being already partially vocalized by another system than
his own, he found certain things anomalous and not con-
formable to the laws of pronunciation current in his time,
and supposed by him to be generally recognizable in the
Old Testament text ; the former being the readings re-
commended by him in these particular cases as sub-
stitutes for the anomalous readings which he found ; the
readings he recommended being conformable to the rules
of pronunciation recognised by him as current in his
day, and supposed by him to prevail generally in the
Scriptures. But, obviously, if the punctuator or voca-
lizer and the original writer of the consonants were one
and the same person such anomalies are totally inex-
plicable ; and as these anomalous words occur in the
latest books of the Old Testament, and there most fre-
quently (*e.g.* Daniel), the punctuation cannot have been
anterior to the close of the Canon.

It may have been contemporary, however, with this
event. But the fact that the vocalizer, whoever he was,
stuck his own vocalization upon consonants which it did
not fit, and did not presume to alter the consonantal
text, makes this supposition unlikely, and renders it
probable that the punctuator did not feel himself to
possess a similar authority to that of the original writers.
In the hands of inspired writers the productions of pre-
vious inspired men are treated with all freedom. None
are so remarkable for this free use of their predecessors
as two of the later writers, Jeremiah and the Chronicler.
They permit themselves the greatest liberties with the
foregoing text, feeling their own divine commission to
warrant any adaptation of previous divine words that

their own times and circumstances may demand. The vocalizers, however, allow themselves no such freedom; they were conscious of standing on a much lower platform than the writers of the consonantal text. Hence any claim that may be put in for Ezra is not to be looked at.

(c) A more conclusive testimony is that of versions. (1) The Septuagint. Here there are two points—the remarkable agreement in many cases between the Septuagint and our present vocalization, and the equally remarkable disagreement in others. Advocates of a preseptuagintal vocalization lay much weight on the former, their opponents equally much on the latter. The latter, the fact of deviation in such a multitude of instances—which we need not cite as any one can lay his hand on many such passages in the Septuagint, which are numerous in proportion to the difficulties of the text, and it is often quite evident *what* punctuation has been supplied to the naked consonants—seems quite conclusive against the existence of vowel signs at the time of this translation. For agreement is explicable from context and especially from tradition; disagreement on the supposition of a pointed text is explicable only on the hypothesis of erroneous punctuation on the part of MSS. employed by the Seventy, or erroneous punctuation on the part of our Masoretic Bibles. The former is improbable, *first*, from the nature of the undertaking, because on any hypothesis of object or translator, the best and correctest MSS. would be at the command of the authors; *second*, the deviations are too wide to be explicable on the ground of different punctuation, they are often the result of sheer conjecture put forth by an ignorance that felt itself completely at a loss. The latter hypothesis, error in our Masoretic Bibles, is a hypothesis destructive of our faith in our present punctuation, and is otherwise not to be entertained, because *per se* the Masoretic readings are widely more rational and self-testifying than those of the Septuagint. But to refer the blunders of the Septuagint to a vocalization at all, destroys our faith in all vocalization. For if such a vocalization existed so early, containing such manifold deviations from another vocalization which has now become current, we give little for either or both. It is satisfactory, however, to know that in Jerome's time the uniform conviction was that the Seventy had no vowels before them; and this Father explains and excuses their mistakes from that fact,—verbi ambiguitate decepti (in Isaiam, xxiv. 23).

(2) The Targums or Chaldee translations. The agreement of Onkelos with our present punctuation is something remarkable. It is hardly fair, however, to assert[6] that hardly any deviations are to be found. There are a good few passages.[7] In Jonathan's Targum on the Prophets the instances are numerous, and all Buxtorff's sophistry[8] cannot explain them away. In the Targum of Pseudo Jonathan on the Pentateuch, or the Targum Jerushalmi, examples meet us everywhere. That Onkelos is more correct than the others arises partly from his own character as a scholar and faithful translator and adherent of his tradition, while the others—even Jonathan, to some extent—are mere paraphrasers, their additions in some cases amounting to actual Midrashim (e.g. on the Song); and partly from the plainness of the law, and the intimate acquaintance, for many reasons, of all Jews with its readings. This latter circumstance, it is, which accounts for the superiority of the Seventy's version of the Pentateuch. It is precisely, as with them, in the difficult passages, such as the song of Jacob, Gen. xlix., that Onkelos hesitates and loses hold of an unwavering tradition. It is a conjecture of Gesenius altogether groundless and intolerable, that the agreement between Onkelos and our own is to be explained by supposing Onkelos the basis of the later punctuation.[9]

---

[6] As does Buxtorff, Tractatus de punct, p 136.
[7] See for examples, Winer de Onkeloso, p. 29 and ff.
[8] Tractat de punct, p 138 ff.
[9] Geschichte der Hebr. Sprache, s. 193

(3) The Peshito Syriac. Here we need not go far to meet with many proofs that this translation was made from unpointed MSS. In Gen. xxii. 14, for example, יִרְאֶה has been read יְרָאֶה, instead of יִרְאֶה. So, Gen. xlix. 24, מִשָּׁם *from there*, has been read and translated מִשֵּׁם from *Shem*.[10]

(*d*) After the acute investigations of Hupfeld already alluded to, it must be conceded that Jerome, however much he knew of vowels and spake of them, knew nothing of our present vowel or accentual signs. He employs the term *accentus*, but not in the sense of accent, but of pronunciation.[11] It must be granted to the same author that the Talmud is also ignorant of vowel or accentual signs in our sense of the word.[12]

(*e*) To all this might be added much more. For example, the historic fact of a change of the form of the consonantal writing long after the close of the canon. Ezra has no claim to be regarded as the author of the present square character, nor has any single individual; that character is the slow result of time, and the operation of the double tendency to tachygraphy and calligraphy, producing on the one hand a rounder and swifter character than the old Phenician, which is stiff and awkward and unconnected, and on the other appending points and corners, or Taggin, by way of ornament. But the present vowels can accommodate themselves only to the present consonants; these cannot have been generally current long before our era, and not exclusively even then, and so the vowels must be more recent still. Again, to the same effect is the unlawfulness of using in the synagogues a pointed text. The consonants alone were holy, the vowels common and unclean and excrescences of mere human growth upon the exclusively divine.

[10] For much information on this and other points connected with this version, see Hirzel, De Pent. vers Syr. quam Peshito vocant, indole, p 12. etc ; Credner, De Proph. Minor vers Syr indole, p 54 f and 91 c.
[11] Hupfeld, Studien u. Kritiken, 1830, p 571   [12] Ibid, p 554

A final argument may be referred to. In 1845, Dr. Pinner, the editor of the " Talmud, with German translation,"[13] published a prospectus and list of MSS. belonging to the Odessa Society for History and Antiquities.[14] The editor divides these MSS. into three classes : A. ספרי תורה, rolls of the law ; B. ספרי תנ״ך, rolls of Biblical books in general, law, prophets, and Hagiographa ; C. ספרי תלמוד וגאונים, Talmudic and rabbinical writings. In the second class, B, and in this class, No. 3—the later prophets—stands a MS. with a vocalization and accentuation widely different from our common Masoretic system. The MS contains the writings of Isaiah, Jeremiah, Ezechiel, and the twelve minor prophets. The vowels and accents in this MS. differ from our own, not only in form and position, but also in number. In position, all the vowels, and nearly all the accents, stand above the line ; in number the accents are fewer, the vowels more numerous, amounting in all to twenty. Pattach furtive does not appear ; and there are no double accents, nor any post-positive or prepositive, but all stand on the tone-syllable.[15] At the same time the vowel and accentual systems are fundamentally the same as those of the Masoretes, agreeing in many cases to the slightest shades. This punctuation must have taken its rise somewhere in the East, and has accordingly been named the Assyrian system.[16] Our pre-

[13] Unfortunately, no more than the first volume ever appeared, death having arrested the progress of the great work

[14] The somewhat lengthy title of Dr Pinner's prospectus is " Prospectus der der Odessaer Gesellschaft für Geschichte n. Alterthümer gehörenden ältesten Hebräischen und rabbinischen Manuscripte, ein Beitrag zur Biblischen Exegese, von Dr. Pinner, Herausgeber des Talmud mit Deutscher Uebersetzung, nebst einem lithographirten Fac-simile des Propheten חבקוק Habaquq, aus einem Manuscripte vom Jahre, 916. Odessa auf Kosten der Gesellschaft, 1845.

[15] Those who have not access to the work of Pinner itself, may consult a good account of it, given by Ewald, Jahrbucher, 1848, p. 160 ff (art. vii.)

[16] Babylon war das Saatfeld für die meisten Gattungen der jüdischen Litteratur. Fürst, Kultur u. Literaturgeschichte der Juden in Asien, p. 2, quoted by Donaldson, Jashar, p. 18, note

sent system is a native of the West, perhaps Tiberias. The MS. in which the Assyrian appears bears date 916. But from inspecting it, it can be seen at once that the particular system with which it is accented was not the only one known to the accentuators, but was beginning to give way before another, the Tiberian. Double punctuation occurs in several cases, and the first three verses of Malachi have been pointed quite according to our mode of punctuation.

These facts seem to indicate, beyond the reach of controversy, that the determination of the Jewish mind in the direction of vocalization and accentuation was not a determination peculiar to the western or Palestinian Jews, but common to them with their eastern or Assyrian countrymen. They show that the mere invention of symbols was a thing of comparatively modern date, and that the symbols took different forms in different regions. They show further that while different families constructed different systems of symbols, and worked independently, though contemporaneously, at giving sensuous form and outward expression to their tradition, it was yet a common tradition which they laboured to express. So that while we cannot hesitate to believe in the comparatively modern rise of our present signs, we have every reason to consider ancient and primitive the pronunciation and declamation which they so successfully signify.[17]

---

[17] See the arguments for the late origin of the punctuation, excellently stated (in addition to the books already mentioned) in Gesenius, Geschichte der Heb Sprache, Abschnitt iii, B, p 182 folg ; Jahn, Einleitung, § 96, s. 340, folg.; also Havernik, Einleitung, i 1, s 304 ff, who borrows from Hupfeld. Also briefly, Horne's Introduction by Davidson, vol ii., p 18 and foll

§ 3. ACCENTUAL SIGNS.

As all words in a sentence must have some logical relation to the words immediately beside them, and that relation can only be of two kinds, that is a relation of connection or a relation of disjunction, Hebrew accents, as expressive of one or other of these relations, are called connectives or disjunctives. The former are also called servants, and the latter domini or lords. These names express their logical power; the names "Hebungen," elevations, and "Senkungen," depressions, are indicative of their rhythmical value as expressing particular modulations of the voice. The prose accents are the following :—

DISTINCTIVES		CONNECTIVES.	
סִלּוּק	Silluq	מֵרְכָא	Mercha.
אֶתְנָח	Athnach . . .	מוּנַח	Munach.
סֶגלְתָּא)	Sgolta		Munach.
שַׁלְשֶׁלֶתוּ)	Shalsheleth with Psiq		No servant or con- [secution.
זָקֵף קָטֹן)	Zaqeph qaton (small)		Munach.
זָקֵף גָּדוֹל)	Z. gadhol (great)		No servant or con- [secution.
טִפְחָא	Tippecha		Mercha.
רְבִיעַ	Rbhia		Munach.
תְּבִיר	Tbhir	דַּרְגָּא	Darga.
זַרְקָא	Zarqa		Munach.
פַּשְׁתָּא)	Pashta	מַהְפָּךְ	Mahpach. [servant.
יְתִיב)	Jthibh . . .		No consecution or

DISTINCTIVES.		CONNECTIVES.
פָּזֵר)	Pazer	Munach.
קַרְנֵי פָרָה)	Qarne pharah . .	יֶרַח בֶּן יוֹמוֹ Jerach [ben Jomo
תְּלִישָׁא גְדוֹלָה	Thsha gdolah . .	Munach.
גֶּרֶשׁ	Geresh	קַדְמָא Qadma.
גֵּרְשַׁיִם	Gershayim (double G.)	Munach.

1. With regard to the relation of these disjunctives and connectives, the ordinary conditions are as above. Mercha serves regularly only Silluq and Tippecha, but in extraordinary circumstances (sec. 12) it forms the servant of Zarqa, Pashta, and Tbhir. Munach serves regularly Athnach, Sgolta, Zaqeph, Rbhia, Zarqa, Pazer, and Thsha; in extraordinary circumstances it serves Geresh and Gereshayim, the latter of which takes no servant or secution in ordinary circumstances. The relation of the word marked with Thsha qtannah תְּלִישָׁא is somewhat doubtful, though it seems to be a sort of loose connection. In general, when the same accent has two forms, the second appearing only when the conditions necessary to the first are not supplied, this second form takes no servant or consecution

2. It will be seen from the above forms that several accents have the same symbol, and are only to be distinguished from each other by their position. In this way are distinguished Pashta disjunctive and Qadma connective, Jthibh disjunctive and Mahpach connective. Pashta stands uniformly on the last letter of a word, and hence, if the word be penacute, Pashta has to be repeated thus אָרֶץ. Qadma, on the contrary, stands on the initial or medial letters, and never appears on the last except in terminations like ךְ, ךָ, etc.

Again, Jthibh, the substitute of Pashta, always is placed before the first vowel of a word, hence appears

only with monosyllables and penacutes: Mahpach, on
the other hand, always follows the vowel whereon lies
the tone. עִי֔ is Jthibh, but עִ֯י Mahpach. The place
of any accent is immediately after the vowel, if below,
or upon the consonant if above, which it accents.[1]

3. Besides the pitch and stress of sounds indicated by
the accents (§ 1), there is another thing to be observed,
viz. the *breadth* or extension of a sound, when a note is
for some reason expanded beyond its natural compass.
This takes place in two cases : *first*, when two accents
related to each other would meet, requiring two words,
but from the accidental nature of the clause only one
word is at hand, then either the two accents will both
stand on the single word, if its syllables be such as to
admit of this, or one accent will disappear and compen-
sation be made by a corresponding extension of the
other which is left. This extension is denoted either
by doubling the sign or by adding Psiq. It takes
place in four cases · Mercha Kphulah (מֵרכָ֡א) or double
Mercha, Gereshayim, or double Geresh (גֵרְשִׁ֞), Zaqeph
Gadhol (זָקֵ֛ף), and Shalsheleth with Psiq. *Second,*
when the word with a connective, for some reason,
rhythmical chiefly, requires a more decided and em-
phatic enunciation than usual, in other words, requires
to be slightly separated from the word on which it leans
for support, a downright stroke, Psiq, is drawn between
the words to indicate this. This servant with Psiq is,
then, in the language of Ouseel, a *minimus.*

4. Many of the names of these accents have arisen
from their form. Thus Sgolta is connected in form with
Seghol, and both derive their name from their common

---

[1] Besides Jthibh, another accent, viz, Tlisha gdholah can appear
only on an initial letter, and hence these two are called *prepositive* accents
Sgolta, Zarqa, and Tlisha Qtannah can stand only on the final letter of a
word, and hence are named *post-positives.* The scruples of these accents
are purely attributable to rhythmical principles, and are quite *illogical.*

resemblance to a bunch of grapes. Shalsheleth, again,
is *chain*, which its symbol resembles; Zarqa is *spout,
tube*, called in the poetic צִנּוֹר of the same signification,
its form suggesting a crooked pipe. Jerach benyomā
resembles the young moon, the " moon a day old,"[2] and
Qarne pharah, or the union of the Tlishas, reminds one
of a cow's head—" cow's horns." Other names are taken
from the meaning and function of the accents. Thus
Silluq is *pause;* Athnach, *breathing;* Zaqeph, *cross,*
elevation ;[3] Tippecha, *palm,* that is expander ; Pashta the
same. Rbhia may have received its name because it
marked the half of the half verse, that is *quarter*, which
it means,[4] or, as others think, from its point being origi-
nally not round but four-cornered. Tbhir is *fracture,*
equal perhaps to *section ;* Mercha, *prolonger.* מָאֲרֵךְ,
מֵרָךְ מַרְכָא, Aphel participle of אָרַךְ, to lengthen.[5]
Qadma, *foregoer,* is named from its position. Tlisha
perhaps means *shield,* to which it has some distant re-
semblance. Geresh, *extrusion,* when preceded by Qadma,
is called Azla אַזְלָא. The servants, with the exception
of Mercha, Qadma, and Yerach, are said all to have
borne the name שׁוֹפָר *trumpet.*[6] Thus Munach, *erect,*
or supported or resting trumpet; Mahpach, *i.e.* מְהֻפָּךְ,
in Hebrew, *inverted* trumpet ; Darga was likewise named
שׁ׳ גַּלְגַּל. Munach was named also שׁ׳ יָשָׁר straight,
upright, etc.[7] Many of the accents had various names,
according to the different views taken of their form, their

[2] In the poetic accentuation this receives the name of *wheel, galgal,* to
which it also bears some likeness.

[3] Though in the Assyrian system its sign is actually a *cross,* which is
most probably its original form, the double dot arising from a desire to
use the dot or point as far as possible either singly or in combination, and
so introduce something like uniformity.

[4] So Ewald Lehrbuch, 210.

[5] The double mercha again is called תְּרֵין חוּטְרִין *two rods.*

[6] Ewald, Lehrb , s 211

[7] Ewald's Lehrbuch, as above

tone, or their consecution.   Thus Shalsheleth was called
the *thunderer* ; Pazer, the *crasher*, etc.[8]

5. The most casual glimpse at the accents shows that
the connectives in general bend in the direction in which
we read, and the disjunctives in the opposite direction, as
naturally was to be expected.   The servants too or de-
pressions are all placed under the line as became them,
with the exception of Qadma and Tlisha Qtannah.
These last two stand above, because the weaker the dis-
junctive, of necessity the stronger the connective propor-
tionately, and in the case of Geresh, which is exceedingly
weak, the conjunctives rise to an almost perfect equality
of strength with it, and therefore stand above.[9]   On the
other hand, all the powerful disjunctives have weak con-
nectives, because the more powerful the stress on any
particular word, so much the more hurried and slight
will be the utterance of the word immediately preceding
it ; a principle which explains the peculiar form of the
construct state in Hebrew.

Again it will be observed that the light-toned disjunc-
tives are placed above, while the heavy-toned stand
below.[10]   The high and heavy notes are thus indicated
by their position, the high commencing at the commence-
ment of the verse or half-verse, the low and heavy
starting with Tbhir and Tippecha, and ending with
Athnach and Silluq in their respective clauses.   In
Hupfeld's estimation the place of the accent as *pre-posi-
tive* or *post-positive* is also of considerable importance ;
an accent of the former kind retracts the word on which
it stands into connection with the words nearer the
beginning of the verse ; an accent of the latter kind
throws it forward into stronger connection with the words

---

[8] Ewald, ibid   See also the various names given by the older Gram-
marians, recounted in תורת אמת p 3 foll

[9] Hupfeld, Studien u. Kritiken, 1837, s 886. The weakness of Geresh
is such that it may altogether fall out and its place be assumed by a mere
servant. See § 12

[10] Hupfeld, ibid, s. 885   Ewald, ut sup. s 212

following. It is, perhaps, rather to be said that something in the peculiar modulation in utterance of these accents requires their position to be pre-positive or the reverse. And on the above theory of Hupfeld's the position of Sgolta a powerful distinctive as a post positive would create an extreme difficulty, a difficulty not in the least removed by his assertion that Sgolta forms a step towards Athnach![11]

6. The accents not being a single conception, nor having sprung up at a single jet, but being the slow elaboration of successive schools of men and successive centuries of time, there is some room for speculating on the form of the first small beginnings and on the processes through which the embryo idea attained to its present complete development. First of all, the verses in their present state are premasoretic, being recognised even by the Mishnah,[12] and doubtless arose during the decline of the pure Hebrew, from the necessity of translating into the vernacular Chaldee, and the expediency in so doing of reading but a small portion at a time that the people might follow and understand. For some time no external sign was employed to indicate the divisions, and the right observation of the pauses was an art to be taught in the schools. No external sign appears in the synagogue rolls nor is alluded to in the Talmud.[13] Hence the first step towards punctuation must have been made in post-talmudic times. But yet the designation of the verse ending, as is now customary, by two dots, must be referred to a time before the invention of our present accentual signs, because at the verse end there is a double accentuation Silluq and Soph Pasuq, similar to the double vocalization. It is possible that somewhat later, the half verses may have been also indicated by Athnach, so that these two are really not accents properly, but signs of interpunction, which, like the primi-

[11] Stud u Krit, as above p 885.
[12] Megillah, c. 4 1, quoted by Hupfeld.
[13] Hupfeld, as above. Grammatik, p 107.

tive vocalic system, the punctuators already found and
worked over or into their own system.[14]

The development of symbols would thus proceed, as
in all Oriental punctuation, from the single point up
to two, three, or a plurality of points, and when the
point was exhausted onward to the straight, bent, or
twisted line. The order would be ＿ ± ˇ Rbhia, Zaqeph,
Sgolta ; Metheg, Mercha, Munach, Mahpach, Geresh,
Pashta, Qadma, Darga, etc. ; and then on to Tbhir, the
union of the line with the point. The middle of the
half verses was first in this way indicated by Rbhia, but
later, when nearer definition became necessary, the
more distant division was in accordance with its power
indicated by a double point, and the most distant in like
manner, and for the same reason with three points.[15]
All this was necessarily the result of much time, much
earnest study, much patient balancing of one part of the
system with another, and was only successful after many
generations had added to it their patient and life-long
contributions. The barbarous mixture of Hebrew and
Chaldee names, of Eastern and Western forms, the con-
flicting punctuation of many passages, the diver-
sity of names for the same accent, the diversity of
the entire accentual systems of the East and West, all
show that the accentuation was at first a thing of small
proportion, that it gradually grew by the accumulated
contributions of Eastern and Western schools, that it
borrowed from Syria and perhaps from Arabia ; that as
it gained in strength, its aim and ambition rose in pro-
portion ; that content at first with indicating the chief
logical divisions, it was at last satisfied only when it
embraced every individual word, and that this complete-
ness was not attained much before Bagdad was taken
by the Turks or Hastings won by William the Con-
queror.

[14] Hupfeld, Stud. u. Krit., p. 879 (1837).
[15] Hupfeld, ibid, s. 882. Ewald, Lehrbuch, § 88, p. 142, etc.

§ 4. INTERPUNCTION.

A piece of composition consists of a certain number
of ideas connected together and succeeding each other.
This extended piece may be broken up into smaller por-
tions, each containing one or more ideas. These smaller
portions are called verses, or, in Hebrew, Psuqim. The
accents are engaged about a verse. They extend no
further than such single division; so soon as a verse is
completely accented the concatenation ends, and with a
new verse the series begins anew and runs its complete
course towards the verse end, and so on over the whole
chapter and whole Bible. If the verse contain more
than one idea or proposition, each of the clauses con-
taining them is terminated by a great disjunctive accent
placed upon the last word of the clause. A verse may
contain *three* such great clauses but no more.

1. A verse may contain one clause only, Exod. xii. 47.

כָּל־עֲדַת יִשְׂרָאֵל יַעֲשׂוּ אֹתוֹ׃

The greatest of all distinguents, Silluq, terminates such
a clause. Silluq is always accompanied by Soph
Pasuq (verse-end), two dots at the end of the word.

2. A verse may contain two chief ideas, and so two
great distinguents.

וַיְחַזֵּק יְיָ אֶת־לֵב פַּרְעֹה וְלֹא שִׁלַּח אֶת־בְּנֵי יִשְׂרָאֵל׃

Here the final clause is closed as before by the greatest
disjunctive Silluq with Soph Pasuq; while the other
clause is terminated by Athnach, the next greatest dis-
tinguent, standing relatively to Silluq as a colon stands
relatively to a period.

3. A verse may seem to contain three such principal

ideas, and so three great disjunctives. Thus Gen. vi., 4,
" the giants were in the earth in those days," etc., where
the third great distinctive *Sgolta* is at days.   It is to
be observed, however, that the clause under the domi-
nion of Sgolta is not really independent, but subordinate
to Athnach's clause ; Sgolta dividing the clause of
Athnach into two portions in the same way as Athnach
itself divides the clause of Silluq—that is, the whole
verse into two portions.[1]

Did Hebrew content itself with merely indicating the
great logical divisions of the verse as above, its accents
would quite resemble our points, but it undertakes a far
more onerous task than this.   It is evident that among
the words in the clauses respectively bounded by these
great distinctives, there must be a certain relation and
subordination of individual words and even small groups
of words.   The influence of this relation and subordina-
tion will not extend beyond the great distinguent, but it
may be felt in a multitude of ways within the govern-
ment of this disjunctive ; in other terms the words that
lie between two such disjunctives may stand relatively
to each other and to the disjunctive bounding them in a
great variety of ways.   Hebrew accentuation under-
takes to indicate this almost infinite complexity of rela-
tion   There will be, however, naturally some room for
free choice on the part of the punctuator. For example, the
first mentioned sentence, Exodus xii. 47, will logically
fall apart into two groups of words, at the word Israel ;
all the congregation of Israel—shall do it. A disjunctive
accent will stand on Israel כָּל־עֲדַת יִשְׂרָאֵל יַעֲשׂוּ אֹתוֹ׃
The accent Tippecha, under Israel, is called the minor
disjunctive to Silluq.   It is here expressive of the logical
relation of the two small groups of words in the sentence

---

[1] The power of Sgolta is a much contested point, some considering it
independent and some subordinating it to Athnach   The latter seem to
entertain the correct opinion against Ewald, Boston, etc.   See section on
clause of Sgolta.

to each other. It is also expressive of the slight
rhythmical halt which the voice naturally makes
before coming to a final pause, just as musicians are
observed to play several notes slower before coming to
a final stop. [2] Hence the rule:

If the clause of Silluq consist of more than one word
there must always be the minor disjunctive Tippecha in
the clause, even though the sense repudiate a distinctive
accent and demand a connective. In such a case the
rhythm overrules the Logic.

Again, in the second passage cited above, it is evident
that in each of the two clauses the words fall naturally
asunder, into two groups. And God hardened—the
heart of Pharaoh; and he let not go—the children
of Israel. The distinction between these halves is
marked in both cases by Tippecha which is the
minor disjunctive to Athnach as well as to Silluq.

וְלֹא שִׁלַּח אֶת־בְּנֵי יִשְׂרָאֵל and וַיְחַזֵּק יְהֹוָה אֶת־לֵב פַּרְעֹה

Here, again, the pause at Athnach is so great, that a
preliminary pause of slighter duration must precede it,
whether the sense demand it or not. Hence the rule:

If Athnach's clause be of more than one word,
Athnach must be preceded by the minor Tippecha, at
the demand of the natural rhythm.

The same, and even a more stringent rule, applies to the
clause of Sgolta. For example, in the passage Gen. vi. 4:
הַנְּפִלִים הָיוּ בָאָרֶץ בַּיָּמִים הָהֵם the distinction must evi-
dently be made at *earth*, on which word the minor disjunc-
tive to Sgolta, viz., Zarqa must stand. In the present
case, sense and rhythm combine, but the rhythm must be
satisfied even at the expense of the sense. For Sgolta
must, in all circumstances, be preceded by its minor
Zarqa, and the clause of Sgolta must be of such a sort

---

[2] In speech before a great rise there is generally a small rise, and be-
fore a great fall a small fall. This is the expression of a principle of order
which lies in nature, and cannot be further traced or accounted for.

as to admit Zarqa—that is, must consist of more than one word. Hence the further rule :

If a clause which would require Sgolta naturally, consist only of one word, Sgolta cannot then appear, its place being supplied by Shalsheleth with Psiq. Genesis xix., 16.

Now it would appear that we have placed on the above sentences the periods, colons, semicolons, and even commas ; but Hebrew punctuation is not satisfied with this, every word must be connected or disjoined, there is no neutrality in the logical relation of words in a clause, and the accentuators have undertaken to point out how every word stands related. Hence *every* word is loaded with an accent either disjunctive or conjunctive, the former separating it from the immediately following word or clause, the latter uniting it to the immediately following word only.

To resume our first sentence : כָּל־עֲדַת יִשְׂרָאֵל יַעֲשׂוּ אֹתוֹ׃

punctuated as it was left, with final pause and preparatory minor disjunctive ; there are still two words unsignalized as to their connection. But, manifestly, each of them is logically connected with the word immediately following, *shall do*, logically conditioning *it*, and *whole congregation* being logically conditioned by *Israel*. Hence each of these words will be marked with the sign of connection, which sign happens to be in the present case one common [3] to the two disjunctives Silluq and Tippecha, viz., Mercha : כָּל־עֲדַת יִשְׂרָאֵל יַעֲשׂוּ אֹתוֹ׃ The

---

[3] This is a point connected with the accents which presents great difficulties. It is evident from the use of different servants, that the servants had not all the same significance , they represented various tones or sets of tones of the voice. It is evident at the same time from the scanty supply of servants, in comparison with disjunctives, that there is less variety of inflection in the wordconnected than in the word separated. This is quite natural, but how precisely such a servant as Mercha should serve both, or stand next both Tippecha and Silluq, disjunctives of such diverse powers, or how Munach should represent a tone coming immediately before Athnach, one of the lowest tones, and before Pazor, the highest, is somewhat mysterious.

clause of Athnach displays the same grouping of the words, and will be similarly pointed וַיְחַזֵּק יְהֹוָה אֶת־לֵב פַּרְעֹה where the servant of Tippecha is as before Mercha, but the servant of Athnach is Munach.

Finally, the clause of Sgolta, from containing an odd number of words, is somewhat more difficult. הַנְּפִלִים הָיוּ בָאָרֶץ בַּיָּמִים הָהֵם *the giants were in the earth in those days.* The minor disjunctive being already placed at earth, there cannot be any doubt that the words *in those days* are logically connected ; hence a servant or connective will stand on *those* בַּיָּמִים הָהֵם viz., Munach, the servant to Sgolta.

More doubtful is the logical relation of the words *the giants were in the earth ;* but a mere glance at the order of the words tells us that the term *giants* is emphatic, because it stands before its verb, whereas in Hebrew the noun follows its verb if no emphasis be indicated. In English, the words read really, *the giants, they were in the earth in those days..* Hence, *giants* is logically or rhythmically marked off by a certain pause from the following words which are thus thrown closely together.

Were in the earth הָיוּ בָאָרֶץ where Munach is again servant to Zarqa. The whole, therefore, stands thus הָיוּ בָאָרֶץ בַּיָּמִים הָהֵם We have still, however, to dispose of the *giants.* The word is emphatic, emphasis implies pause, so the word will be marked by a pausal or disjunctive accent. But from what shall we disjoin *giants ?* From *were in the earth ?* or from *were in the earth in those days ?* In other words, will the disjunctive which we mean to put on *giants* be a disjunctive standing in relation to Zarqa or to Sgolta ? We have simply to ascertain the proper logical bearing of the passage. Something is to be said of the *giants :* is it *in those days* that is said of them, or is it *in the earth* that is said of them ? Obviously it is that they were on the earth, and

what is said of the giants on the earth, is, that it was in
those days.

    The giants,

    The giants, were on the earth ;

    The giants, were on the earth ; in those days.

That is, the clause *giants* is subordinate to the clause,
were on the earth ; and the combined clause *the giants
were on the earth*, is subordinate to the clause *in those
days*. We punctuate *giants*, therefore, with a distinctive,
having relation to Zarqa הַנְּפִלִים הָיוּ בָאָרֶץ the accent
being Gereshayim or double Geresh, the minor distinc-
tive to Zarqa. In the same manner all other clauses are
punctuated. An example may be taken, introducing
what is called the major disjunctive, Gen. ii., 2. "And
God finished on the seventh day his work which he had
made; and he rested on the seventh day from all his
work which he had made."

Plainly enough the middle of the verse is at *made ;*
that word will therefore bear upon it the sign of the
half verse, Athnach. Each of these two great clauses,
bounded by Silluq and Athnach respectively, will be
independently pointed, and the words will assume posi-
tions of relation only to the words within their own
clause respectively. Taking up the clause proper of
Silluq, *and he rested on the seventh day from all his
work which he had made*: here, at first sight, the
words fall asunder into two groups, *he rested on the
seventh day*, and, *from all his work which he had
made.* Hence a great distinguent will be placed on
day, viz., Zaqeph, the major under Silluq at *made*.

וַיִּשְׁבֹּת בַּיּוֹם הַשְּׁבִיעִי מִכָּל־מְלַאכְתּוֹ אֲשֶׁר עָשָׂה׃

Again, in the group nearest the end it is evident that
the logical order will be, from all his work—which he
had made ; imposing a connective on *which* and a dis-
junctive on *work*, thus, מִכָּל־מְלַאכְתּוֹ אֲשֶׁר עָשָׂה׃ So in
the first group the order will be, and he rested—on

day the seventh; day and seventh being connected, and consequently *rested* being disjoined from them, thus : וַיִּשְׁבֹּת בַּיּוֹם הַשְּׁבִיעִי where the accent on *rested* is Pashta, the minor to Zaqeph on *seventh*. The words form themselves into groups thus, counting backwards from Silluq,

Which he had made.
From all his work, which he had made.
And he rested on the seventh day; from all his work, which he had made.

It is especially to be observed that the influence of any accent extends as far as to that accent under which it immediately stands, or to which it is related in the degree of minor, maximus, major, etc. For instance, the accent on work is minor to Silluq, and therefore its influence extends to Silluq; the connection therefore is not

His work which; but,
His work which he had made.

So again Zaqeph on *day* (or seventh in Hebrew) is major to Silluq, and its influence extends as far as Silluq, in other words, to *made*. So, it is not,

He rested on the seventh day from all his work; but,
He rested on the seventh day from all his work which he had made.

A somewhat peculiar passage will illustrate this. Is. i. 21, is, in our translation, " How is the faithful city become an harlot ! *it was full of judgment; righteousness lodged in it; but now murderers.*" This rendering is not strictly accurate, because *full* is an adjective, and in construction—the *full of judgment*. It matters nothing whether we translate the next clause *righteousness lodged in it*, or relatively, *in which righteousness lodged*, the parallelism will be the same.

How has become an harlot,
The city that was faithful !
Full of jugdment, righteousness lodging in her ;
But now murderers.

Here the opposition is apparent at once, being between
harlot and *faithful*, in the first half, and between the
idea of *justice*, expressed doubly, and *murderers* in the
other member of the verse. In the second member,
therefore, the greatest accent ought to stand on *her*.
The expression, *full of judgment*, forming along with
the group *righteousness lodged in her*, the description of
the former condition of the city and the proper balance
to the clause, *but now murderers*. This, however, is not
the usual punctuation seen in Hebrew Bibles, common
editions setting the chief point at *judgment*, and causing
the parallelism to stand thus—

Full of judgment ;
Righteousness lodging in her, but now murderers:

ruining thereby the parallelism of sense entirely. In
the Edition of Michaelis this is rectified, and the
parallelism of accent is made to harmonise with the
parallelism of sense which ought always to be the case.

מְלֵאֲתִי מִשְׁפָּט צֶדֶק יָלִין בָּהּ

וְעַתָּה מְרַצְּחִים:

In common editions, instead of the Rbhia on *judgment*,
an accent subordinate to the Tippecha on *her*, there
stands a Zaqeph on *judgment*, an accent subordinate
only to Silluq.

A few general principles may here be stated.

The distinguents are divided into great and small, the
great standing at the end of great clauses, the small
standing in subordination to these at the close of smaller
clauses. In punctuating, it is best, first of all, to set
down the two greatest, Silluq at the end and Athnach
in the middle of the verse, and if there seems to be a
third proposition under Athnach, it is to be marked with
Sgolta on its last word. In punctuating single clauses,
the same logical process is to be observed.

Distinctives, according to their power and relation to
another distinctive, are called minors, majors, maximi,

etc. Accents of less distinctive power than the minors are named minimi, which in Prose are less frequent than in Poetry, and have generally no proper independent sign, being usually a mere repetition or some other combination of servants. It will seldom happen that all these various grades will occur in any single verse.

It is of consequence to remark that the *order* of occurrence of the distinctives is unchangeable, viz., minor. major, maximus from end towards beginning of the verse. Some powers may be omitted, but a great power never stands before a less in the same clause.[4] Thus counting from the place of Silluq, its distinguents should stand— minor, Tippecha; major, Zaqeph; maximus, Athnach. It is not necessary that all should appear, but the order must not be confused, so as to put the major before the minor, or the maximus before the major, if they both actually occur.

After placing a great distinguent and another—the minor—relatively to it, if there are still several words unexhausted, it will depend on the logical relation of the words whether new distinguents will be placed relatively to the first great distinguent or relatively to the small distinguent already placed in subordination to the greater one. For example, Gen. i., 14, in the clause of Athnach, *to divide between the day and the night.*

לְהַבְדִּיל בֵּין הַיּוֹם וּבֵין הַלָּיְלָה

If we take the four last words, the disunion falls naturally at *day*, which will assume the minor Tippecha, and *between* in both cases will be marked by a servant, thus

בֵּין הַיּוֹם וּבֵין הַלָּיְלָה

there still remains לְהַבְדִּיל to designate logically. Is, then, the relation thus?

---

[4] A few cases occur of apparent inversion. See sections on Pashta, Zarqa, and Tbhir, whose minors and majors are sometimes transposed.

To divide,
To divide, between the day ;
To divide, between the day ; and between the night
or is it the following?
To divide;
To divide ; between the day and between the night.
It is evidently the latter, for there are only two notions, *division* and *day and night*. The idea *divide* is not subordinate to *day* merely, but to the whole expression *day and night*, since division or separation implies at least two things separated ; that is, divide will be punctuated relatively to the accent on *night*, at the end of the whole expression.

לְהַבְדִּיל בֵּין הַיֹּם וּבֵין הַלָּיְלָה

the accent being Zaqeph Gadhol, the greater distinguent to Athnach.

Hence will be understood the other great principle, that Hebrew punctuation is relative, not absolute. [5] It does not give absolute sense, but relative subordination of idea. It may give sense, but it of necessity gives relative subordination. And the question to be asked in setting down a distinguent greater or less, is not. does the clause over which this distinguent is to preside, give absolute or unconnected meaning of itself? but do these distinctives, etc., indicate fairly the proper relative subordination of clauses to the verse, of clausules to the clause, of words to the clausule, and so on?

Several accents are capable of repetition, that is, two or more of the same accent may appear together under the government of the same great disjunctive. In such cases the second or *repetitus*, that is, the accent nearest the beginning of the verse is of greater distinctive and pausal power than the same accent which stands nearer the end. If it be repeated three times it increases in power each time toward the commencement of the stanza.

---

[5] Against Boston and the older accentuists, who maintained that the accents gave absolute sense

And thus the *repetitus* is not dependent on any inter-
mediate accent but on the great distinguent at the end
of the clause, so that its influence extends over one or
more accents of the same name with itself standing
nearer the end of the verse. Gen. viii. 3, *and the
waters abated at the end of a hundred and fifty days.*

וַיַּחְסְרוּ הַמַּיִם מִקְצֵה חֲמִשִּׁים וּמְאַת יוֹם׃

The accent on *waters* extends over the same accent on
end, making the relation thus—

> And the waters abated ;
> At the end, of a hundred and fifty days.[6]

The series of words under the power of an accent are
said to form the *ditio* or government of the accent. An
accent always stands on the last word of its *ditio*, that
is, the word nearest the end of the verse ; and the words
preceding it towards the beginning are all under its
influence, and every accent placed on them is placed
relatively to the great accent on the last word, mediately
or immediately. The *ditio* of an accent extends toward
the beginning of a verse until the occurrence of an
accent greater than itself (which greater accent, how-
ever, may be itself *repetitus*), where its authority ends
and the next set of words are under the government of
this new ruler, whose territory extends either to the
beginning of the verse or till another greater accent
presents itself. It thus happens that a great distinctive
rules a *ditio* under which are several subordinate ditiones,
under the authority of lesser distinctives.

Considering that the Hebrew accentuation is a sensuous
declamation, an oratory not for the ear but the eye, to
appreciate it aright will have on us the same effect as if
we heard a living voice declaiming the Bible in tones
perfectly natural and perfectly expressive. Those who
understand it will feel how far even the marvellous
melody and meaning of our English falls below it, and
how much more expressive our translation would have

---

[6] The first verse in Isaiah furnishes a good example.

been had it adhered with more fidelity in its punctuation
to the Hebrew. Thus in Is. i. 2, our version points,
" Hear, O heavens ; and give ear, O earth : for the Lord
hath spoken, I have nourished," etc. The Hebrew runs,
Hear Heavens ! and give ear Earth ! for *Jehovah*, hath
spoken : I have nourished, etc. The English by putting
the chief accent at earth and only a comma at spoken,
loses the fine idea of the original (which puts the chief
pause at *spoken*), that Heaven and Earth must hear
simply because *Jehovah* hath spoken. The speaker de-
mands attention independently of what he says. Hence
the Masoretes, with fine appreciation, put the chief pause
at *spoken*, and another pause at Jehovah, which last is
equivalent to our underlining or emphasis in utterance.

A pretty instructive example occurs Genesis, vi. 17,
which runs thus in our translation : " Behold I, even I,
do bring *a flood of waters upon the earth*." This transla-
tion is in defiance, first, of the accentuation ; second, of
one of the best known rules of Hebrew syntax, viz., that
a noun in construction never admits the article ;[7] and,
third, of the analogy offered by chap. vii. 6, where,
however, our translators, determined to have their fa-
vourite "flood of waters" promoted, bring the words
flood and *waters* into the genitive relation though they
be actually separated by a verb and a semicolon,
הַמַּבּוּל הָיָה מַיִם וְגוּ—the flood was—waters upon the
earth. Except once or twice the word מַבּוּל stands
always as a definite noun with the article, and the phrase
מַבּוּל מַיִם " flood of waters." does not occur, but instead
of it מֵי הַמַּבּוּל, waters of the flood ; and the expression
מַיִם עַל הָאָרֶץ is only an exegetical gloss for the purposes
of explanation, " Noah was six hundred years old when

---

[7] A few exceptions proving the rule are met with, *e g* הַמֶּלֶךְ אַשּׁוּר
where the second noun being a proper name cannot, according to the rule,
take the article, and hence it is thrown upon the first, a very emphatic
definition of the person being expressed.

the flood was—waters upon the earth." "Behold I do bring the flood,—waters upon the earth ; to destroy," etc.

It is to be expected, seeing our translation gives the general sense so accurately, that it will be only finer shades of meaning that the study of the accents will supply ; yet these finer shades give generally the acutest pleasure to a cultivated reader or exegete. In Job xiv. 7, our translation reads. "For there is hope of a tree if it be cut down that it will sprout again." The Masoretic accentuation is—

For a *tree* hath hope :
If it be cut down, then it will sprout again . . .
But man dieth, and wasteth away, etc.

There is something more hopeless and pathetic in putting the first line categorically and not hypothetically as our Bible does ; and then, in addition, the Masoretes strongly accent tree, which we can only do in writing by under-lining.

A more palpable case might be found in the same Book, chap. ix. 19. "If *I speak* of strength ; lo, *he is strong:* and if of judgment, who shall set me a time *to plead*," the words "I speak" not being in the Hebrew. Here the first member of the verse has evident reference to God, but the second seems to refer to Job himself, which is extremely unlikely from the regularity of the parallelism in this Book. At any rate, the first member is translated, both in contradiction to the accents and in contradiction to the usage of הִנֵּה which stands first in its clause with no word before it. According to the accents, the words *strength* and *strong* are a genitive relation—if I speak of strength of the strong—lo ! But plainly the word lo ! is an interjection supposed to come from God himself, and might be more expressively rendered here ! or here I am !

Is it a question of strength,—"Here I am !" (He cries.)
A question of law, " Who will implead me ?"

The Deity is felt by Job to be too much for him in any

encounter. If he thinks to confront him with force, the Almighty is ready and willing for aught in that way; if he would take the law of Him, where is the man or the court that will venture to sist Him?

A very singular specimen of bidding defiance to accent is to be found in Psalm xlv., 5, running so in our version. "Thine arrows are sharp in the heart of the king's enemies; *whereby* the people fall under thee." This rendering not only defies the accents but permits itself to invert the entire order of the stanza, by drawing the first and last clauses together, and by their pressure extruding altogether the middle clause, which is brought up at the end under the ignominious leading of the halter *whereby*. In Hebrew the greatest pause is at *sharp* or *sharpened*, being the Passive Part.; the next greatest at *thee*, and the final stop at *king;* reading thus—

Thine arrows are sharp:—
Peoples fall under thee!—
In the heart of the enemies of the king!

Does it need a very powerful imagination to see a whole campaign here? A warrior—who is the fairest of the sons of men, but yet the Mighty God—is seen stalking into the field with sharpened weapons,—the same, mowing down nations,—fields of slain, each with a well-aimed javelin in his heart! The poets imagination outruns his power of expression, and makes his picture hurried and irregular. He *sees* scene follow scene with the rapidity of lightning, and utters a hasty half-broken exclamation at each new step in the warrior's progress,—the preparation, the conflict, the victory.[8]

[8] Hence the intolerable nature of all those translations which supply any connective words, or paraphrase in any way this most graphic passage. For example, De Wette, and even Ewald, from whose taste, if not fidelity, something better might have been looked for, supply the verb *dringen*, scharf dringen deine Pfeile, Ew. Deine scharfen Pfeile—dringen, De W. Even Hupfeld's exposition is liable to the same objection, and only Delitzsch, as usual, has delicacy enough to realize what is expressed by the original.

And nothing is more surprising than the complete-
ness with which the Masoretic punctuators enter
into the spirit of the passage, and, indeed, did no
example but the present exist of their fidelity and fine
taste, it would be enough to induce us to put our-
selves almost completely under their direction. In
order well to express the rapidity and almost terrified
breathlessness with which the last two exclamations in
this verse are to be uttered, these Masoretes dispense
with one of the commonest rules of their prosody, viz.,
that under Athnach there must be a long and pausal
vowel, and allow here a simple Sheva יִפְלוּ.

Under this general head of *feeling*, two species of
punctuation deserve to be noticed—*emphatic* punctua-
tion and *pathetic* punctuation. To express emphasis,
slowness and firmness of utterance is necessary. Hence
in emphatic punctuation, accents of greater weight will
be employed than in ordinary discourse, servants will
become minimi, minors rise into majors, majors will be
repeated or turn into maximi. The clausules will be
short and decided, and thus solemnity and dignity con-
tributed to the delivery. Thus Hosea vi. 10 :

בְּבֵית יִשְׂרָאֵל רָאִיתִי שַׁעֲרוּרִיָּה

in the house of *Israel !*
I have seen—a horrible thing,

the greatest pause is at *Israel*, where there is an inten-
tional break to keep Israel, with all its divine environ-
ment and all the history which the name suggested, as
long as possible before the mind. Then another pretty
great pause at seen, but represented by a dash, as if the
speaker hesitated and trembled to utter the last word—a
horrible thing. In ordinary delivery, such a clause
would have stood punctuated thus

בְּבֵית יִשְׂרָאֵל רָאִיתִי שַׁעֲרוּרִיָּה

The second variation from the plain accentuation may
be called the *impassioned*. This style is the reverse of

the last, being designed to indicate rapidity and pas-
sionate utterance. Hence accents of *less* power will be
employed than in ordinary circumstances ; minors will
become servants, majors become minors, which, in some
circumstances, may be repeated ; the words will be
hurried, and come thick in succession, with hardly any
pause between. There may also be frequent use of the
Maqqeph binding several words into one. An example
of impassioned punctuation is found in Is. i. 4.

עָזְבוּ אֶת־יְהוָֹה נִאֲצוּ אֶת־קְדוֹשׁ יִשְׂרָאֵל נָזֹרוּ אָחוֹר׃

They have forsaken the Lord, they have provoked the
Holy One of Israel to anger, they are gone away back-
ward. All the accents are small, the greatest being at
anger.

Another example may be given from the next verse.

עַל־מֶה תֻכּוּ עוֹד תּוֹסִיפוּ סָרָה

The English translation is somewhat against the accentua-
tion as well as the syntax.—Why should ye be stricken
any more? Ye will revolt more and more ; for the
accentuation gives but one *idea* in the clause, but the
idea is compound, containing two conceptions, *stricken
more* and *revolt more* ; but these are made to coalesce,
thus : Why should ye be stricken any more, revolting
more and more ? This, indeed, is the rendering of the
Seventy, προστιθεντες ανομιαν ; and of the Vulgate,
addentes prævaricationem ; and is approved by Ewald
and Drechsler.[9]

Thus, to resume the chief facts of interpunction, the
end of a verse is marked by Silluq, the middle of a verse
by Athnach, the middle of Athnach's clause, or, at least,
the greatest division in it, by Sgolta. Silluq and
Athnach cannot appear without Tippecha to introduce
them, nor Sgolta without Zarqa. If the immediate
clause of Silluq, that is the series of words extending

---

[9] Ewald, Propheten des Alt. Bundes, i s. 245, " ferner sündigend '
Drechsler, Der Proph. Jesaia, s, 53, " mehrend Abfall." See their respec-
tive notes.

from the verse end to Athnach, be divisible into two
chief clauses, this division is effected by the major
Zaqeph. So precisely with the clause of Athnach. If,
again, this half clause under Zaqeph is to be subdivided,
the division is effected by Rbhia (see table § 5), etc. In
this way there is seldom any ambiguity in sense as there
is in English, because the accents being not absolute but
relative, and their relations well defined and unchange-
able, it is at once seen in what relation they stand, and
how far their influence extends. Hence no principle is
of such importance in Hebrew accentuation as the prin-
ciple that the influence of an accent extends as far as the
great accent under which it is immediately placed. In
English, for example, the passage, "There is no peace,
saith my God, to the wicked," Is. lvii. 21, is quite
ambiguous. It may mean, there is no peace to 'the
wicked, saith my God—speaking of them; or there is
no peace, saith my God to the wicked—speaking to
them. The former is the sense generally extracted from
the English, the latter is the meaning presented by the
accentuation.

אֵין שָׁלוֹם אָמַר אֱלֹהַי לָרְשָׁעִים׃

Where the accent on *peace*, viz., Zaqeph is one that
stands in immediate relation to Silluq, and thus puts
the clause which it bounds in co-ordination to the
remaining words after it, thus—

אֵין שָׁלוֹם
אָמַר אלהי לָרְשָׁעִים׃

" No peace !"
Saith my God to the wicked.

It is a defiance and proclamation of eternal war between
Him and them, which God throws down before the
wicked.

Sometimes, indeed, as in the well known passage,
Hab. ii. 4, *the just shall live by his faith*, some doubt

may arise, because the distinctives are employed to *emphasise*, that is to accent rhythmically, when there is no proper logical or·syntactical distinction.   The present case

וְצַדִּיק בֶּאֱמוּנָתוֹ יִחְיֶה

looked at superficially, reads : The just by his faith shall live ; and not, the just shall live by his faith.   But if the accentuator meant to emphasise *faith*, as being in any way the principle of life, he had no means of accomplishing his end, but by putting a disjunctive on *faith*. So that, curiously enough, the passage is left ambiguous, as it is in Greek, even by the accentuation, though there is little doubt from the context that our English rendering is correct.   The ambiguity of the Hebrew could be preserved by writing thus, the just by his *faith* shall live. [10]

[10] Some prefer to put the Tippecha or disjunctive on צַדִּיק. See Mich. Heb. Bib note on the passage.   According to him, four Erfurt MSS., the Ed. of Bomberg, Venice, 1618 ; of Buxtorf, Basle, 1620, the Antwerp Ed., 1571 ; the Ed. of R. Stephens, Paris, 1546 ; the English Polyglot, and some others, place the Tippecha on this word.   See the common punctuation defended, Hitzig : die 12 kleinen Propheten, s. 260, and especially the exegetically exquisite commentary of Delitzsch on Hab., s. 50, where the common meaning is shewn to be quite consistent with the common punctuation.

§ 5. TABLE OF PROSE ACCENTUATION.

ANALYSIS.

1.   The lines marked I., II., etc., represent the Disjunctives, the intermediate lines form their respective connectives.

2.   II. contains the minors of the *opposite* accents in I., and the last accent on II. is the common major to those in I.

3.   III. contains the minors to the *opposite* accents in II., and the last accent in III. is the common major to those in II.

4.   The consecution at the back of the vinculum is the proper consecution of Rbhia, but is common to it with all the accents in III., which is indicated by the vinculum.

5.   The oblique stroke drawn to the Qadma, the servant of Geresh, indicates that the Geresh may itself be omitted, and the consecution commence with Qadma. When Geresh is so omitted after any of the accents in III., the servant of III. will be found invariably present, and this servant will then assume the functions of Geresh, standing as a very slight disjunctive. The reason of the omission of Geresh is, that the two clauses

slide into each other, and in this way extrude the disjunctive, the sense demanding hardly any pause.

6. The consecution with or without Geresh, common to the accents in III., may proceed in either of two ways. If, after [1] Qadma, the servant of Geresh, there be a word pretty closely related to the word marked with Qadma or Geresh, it will take upon it Tlisha Qtannah; if there follow several more toward the beginning of the verse, all more or less closely related, they will each take Munach, or, if one be slightly disjoined, a Psiq may be inserted to indicate the disjunction. If, however, a real distinction be required between Tlisha Qtannah and the beginning of the verse, this distinction is made by Pazer. If there still stand between Pazer and the commencement of the verse a number of words, each will take Munach if they are connected; if a slight disjunction is necessary, a Psiq may be used with one of the Munachs; if considerable disjunction be required, Pazer will be repeated with the same following as before. This process seems to go on under the dominion of Geresh, so that we have Geresh, minor Tlisha Qtannah, major Pazer, repeated if necessary. [2]

7. But supposing we wanted to carry on the consecution under the government of III., to which Geresh serves as common minor: then, as major to III. we put Tlisha Gdolah, which has the same consecution as T. Qtannah; that is, a series of connected words will each take Munach, if there be a slight distinction or emphasis on one it will insert a Psiq; but if there be a great distinction, Pazer will be used, which follows the same course, taking Munach or Munach Psiq, or, if necessary, repeating itself and again going through the same course, the Pazer being repeatable five times. The process, therefore, is III., Geresh minor to III., Tlisha Gdolah major to III., Pazer maximus to III.

[1] That is nearer the beginning of the verse
[2] It is somewhat difficult to define the relation of the word marked by Tlisha Qtannah.

8. Instead of Pazer may be used the conjunction of the Tlishas, called Qarne-pharah or Great Pazer. This compound accent carries with it the same consecution as the simple Pazer, except that the word next it must have under it Yerach ben Yomo; the rest will assume Munach or Munach Psiq if necessary, and as Qarne-pharah does not bear repetition, if repetition be necessary, Pazer will be the major repetitus. The Masorah reckons 16 cases [3] where Great Pazer is employed. See Joshua xix., 51, for a very instructive consecution.

The above table presents the most general features of the prose system. For fuller details and exceptional cases, the following sections must be consulted.

[3] See Nordheimer's Heb. Grammar, vol. ii., p. 342, note.

§ 6. CLAUSE OF SILLUQ.

ANALYSIS.

1. The servant or connective (or if the name be preferred, Depression) to Silluq is always Mercha. Bible *passim*.

2. If the word next Silluq be accompanied by a slight pause, a Psiq will be inserted between the two words. Exod. xvi. 5, Mercha Psiq is then in the nomenclature of Ouseel and others, called the minimus of Silluq.

3. The minor to Silluq is Tippecha. Bible *passim*. This minor necessarily occurs if the clause be of more than one word. (§ 4.)

Occasionally Silluq assumes Tippecha upon its own word; Tippecha then takes the place of Metheg. Levit. xxi. 4. The Masorah on this passage records that five such cases occur. Numb. xv. 21; Isai. viii. 17; Hosea xi. 6; 1 Chron. ii 53; but the diversity in Edd. is extraordinary.[1]

4. The major to Silluq is Zaqeph, Gadhol or Qaton. The former can be employed only in clauses of one word, that is, admits neither servant nor consecution. This major Zaqeph cannot occur unless the minor Tippecha be already present, but may be repeated. It is found once, Gen. i. 2; twice, Gen. iii. 17; three times, Gen. iii. 1; four times, 2 Sam. xvii, 9. It is remarked

---

[1] See these cases discussed Ouseel, p. 365; Spitzner, p. 123, Nordheimer ii., p. 335 note.

by Ouseel that this repetition is rare unless Athnach be present in the verse, and not exceeding twice in the absence of this accent. [2]

5 The parenthesis marks the termination of Silluq's clause. If the verse contain another great clause, this latter is always under the government of Athnach, that is, Athnach stands on its last word and all its accents are placed relatively to it, mediately or immediately. Only *two* places occur where Sgolta takes the place of Athnach. Job i. 8 ; Ezra vii. 13. [3] Spitzner accounts for this last passage by supposing that Sgolta occupies its proper place in the clause, that Athnach should have fallen on the penultimate word, which it might have done had not the last word been monosyllabic, but this circumstance caused Tippecha to assume the place of Athnach—an explanation which shews that the thing is inexplicable.

It is hardly necessary to say that the above skeleton outline of Silluq's clause contains only the servant of Silluq, and the accents placed immediately with reference to Silluq. There will, in all probability, be a great many more words than three or four in Silluq's clause, but the other words will be only mediately under Silluq, and immediately under the influence of Silluq's distinctives, Tippecha and Zaqeph. This remark applies to all the outlines that are to follow.

[2] Chapter iv., p 48.
[3] Ouseel, chap. iv , p 83. Ewald takes no notice of the passage in Ezra, and explains the passage in Job as a mistake, from Job ii 3, where the same words occur and with the same accents, Athnach, however, being also present in the verse—" Ijob 1 8, muss sich aus 2, 3 ein Fehler eingeschlichen haben " Giam , p 186 *note* The same explanation had already been offered by Spitzner, p 125

§ 7. CLAUSE OF ATHNACH.

ANALYSIS

1. Servant to Athnach is Munach. Bible *passim*.

2. If the word next Athnach's word would have a slight pause upon it, Psiq is inserted between it and Athnach's word. Gen. xviii. 15, 21 : and often. Suppose two words require to be joined to Athnach's word, each of them will take Munach. The rhythm cannot, however, tolerate long words here, no case occurs where both words bearing Munach are not monosyllables.[1] See Exod. iii. 4 ; xii. 39 ; Numb. xxii. 36 ; 1 Sam. xvii. 39 ; xxvii. 13. 2 Sam xii 19 ; 1 Kings xxi. 16, etc. In Ezek. viii. 6, a curious case occurs מֵהֶם, both Munachs resting on one word, the Qri, however, is מֵהֶם. Munach Psiq and Munach Munach are called by Ouseel *minimi* ; whether they are to be so called or whether they are servants is merely a question of nomenclature. [2]

The following cases are to be noted where Munach appears on the same word as Athnach. Gen. xxx. 11 ; Hosea vii. 15 ; 1 Chron. v. 20. In the first passage, the

---

[1] The case Deut xxxi 23 אֲשֶׁר נִשְׁבַּעְתִּי לָהֶם is more correctly written with Maqqeph אֲשֶׁר־ leaving room for only one Munach.

[2] Spitzner lays down the canon : Servi duo pluresve, suo, non vicario officio, juxta se positi, nullibi apparent : In which case some one of two servants must appear, not as servant, but as distinctive (p. 107) On the other side, Boston, chap xii, Apud me quidem nihil habet dubitationis quin officium ministrorum *conjunctivum* sit *perpetuum* plane et in- variatum, &c

Qrī recommends the pronunciation of two words.   In
ordinary circumstances, a Metheg would be found in-
stead of the Munach.

3.   The minor to Athnach is Tippecha, subject to
exactly the same conditions as in the case of Silluq;
that is, if Athnach's clause consist of more than one
word, Tippecha must be employed.   Bible *pass*.   It is
noted by the Masorah that Tippecha occurs *eleven* times
on the same word with Athnach.   Numbers xxviii. 26;
Jerem. ii. 31; Ezek. x. 13; in the other eight cases the
word is compound.   Gen. viii. 18; 2 Kings ix. 2;
Ezek. vii. 25; xi, 18; Ruth i. 10; Dan. iv. 9 and 18;
2 Chron. xx. 8.[3]   The printed Edd. present extraor-
dinary variety.   In Hahn's Ed. of Vander Hooght only
the first two and last cited passages exhibit the pecu-
liarity, while the third passage has Metheg, and all the
others are printed separately.

4.   The major to Athnach is Zaqeph, precisely as in
the case of Silluq, and subject to the same laws.   It
may be repeated as often as four times, and when re-
peated is often followed by Sgolta.   If repeated four
times, Sgolta always appears except in one passage.
2 Chron. viii. 13.[4]

The parenthesis marks the close of Athnach's clause.
The question whether Sgolta be an accent under Ath-
nach or co-ordinate with Athnach is not of great im-
portance, though the former view is most probably the
correct one.   Practically the influence of Athnach ends
with Sgolta, which cannot be repeated, and has its own
peculiar consecution.   Spitzner and Ouseel subordinate
Sgolta to Athnach, the former holding the accentual
principle to be a Dichotomy.   Ewald, who believes the
accentual principle to be a Trilogy, maintains the inde-
pendence of Sgolta.   Boston is, as usual, emphatic
Sgolta est Dominus *primarius*, Athnacho minime infe-
rior, verum *par* dignitate, p. 95.

[3] See Ouseel, p 365-6; Spitzner § 158.
[4] Spitzner § 148. Ouseel, p. 182.

§ 8 CLAUSE OF SGOLTA.

ANALYSIS

1. Sgolta cannot occur without its minor Zarqa. If
the nature of the passage be such that Sgolta is logically
required on a word which is the first word of the verse,
Sgolta necessarily gives place to its representative
Shalsheleth with Psiq [1] The sound of this accent is
a circumflex or triple shake, which is indicated by its
figure. Gen. xix. 16; xxiv. 12; xxxix. 8; Lev. viii. 23;
Is. xiii. 8, Amos i. 2.; Ezra v. 15—are the passages noted
by the Masorah.

2. The servant of Sgolta is Munach. Bible *pass.*
Should two words be connected with Sgolta, both will
take Munach. If a slight pause should be expressed
before the Sgolta, a Psiq may be added to the Munach,
with this condition, however, that the third word also
invariably has Munach.[2] Instead of the Munach on
the third word, some Edd. occasionally write a Mercha.
See Gen. iii. 14, in various editions. For two Munachs

[1] That Shalsheleth is the substitute of Sgolta was perceived so early
as by Schindler, and is fully recognised by Spitzner, § 152, Ewald
Lehrbuch, p 188, 3; and Nordheimer, p. 336 The elder accentuists,
such as Ouseel, considered it the substitute of Rbbia; but if the substitute
of Rbbia, no good reason can be given why Rbbia itself should not appear,
since it can stand in a clause of one word, and on the first word in a verse.
It is remarkable that Tregelles should be ignorant of all this. Heads,
p 118.
[2] Ouseel, p 185 and 354

without Psiq, see Gen. xxii. 9 ; Exod. xvi. 29 , with Psiq, Gen. xxvi. 28.

3. The minor of Sgolta is Zarqa, which is necessarily connected with Sgolta, and may appear on the word next that accent or be removed to the fourth word when Munach accents the second and third words. This minor may be repeated three times, 2 Kings i. 16. According to Onseel, when Zarqa is repeated twice or thrice, the major always follows.

4. The major to Sgolta is Rbhia, which is capable of repetition. This repetition is uncommon, and extends only to twice, 1 Sam. xvi. 10 ; except in the double punctuation of the Decalogue, Exod. xx. Deut. v., where Rbhia occurs, thrice repeated. Should there be a necessity for a fourth repetition, which Rbhia never admits, Zaqeph is used in the fourth instance, which has been indicated by placing it below the position which the fourth Rbhia would occupy, Exod. xx. 2; Deut. v. 6. Some prefer to call Zaqeph maximus to Sgolta in such a position.

Different from this is the use of Zaqeph, as the substitute of Rbhia. Three passages are thus punctuated, 1 Sam. xi. 11 ; the otherwise irregular passage, Job i. 8 ; and 2 Chron. xiv. 7. Zaqeph may here be called maximus to Sgolta as before. It is, perhaps, chiefly a question of name, although, of course, there could be no reason for using Zaqeph instead of Rbhia, unless a greater distinction or another modulation than Rbhia's were intended to be marked, but whether it be a greater pause or a different modulation, or both, seeing modulation is the concomitant of pause, it is of no great consequence to discover.

Another peculiarity in the clause of Sgolta is the substitution of Pashta for Rbhia. This usage is subject to conditions which are the reverse of the conditions under which Zaqeph takes Rbhia's place. *First*, Pashta never occurs except when there is a repetition of the Rbhia ; and *second*, Pashta has never any consecution or servant.[3] These facts seem to afford some explanation of the usage, the principle of which is, perhaps, this : the laws of inflection do not permit two Rbhias to stand in immediate proximity. If the logical division would require such interpunction, the logic must give way and one Rbhia is replaced by Pashta.[4]

[3] One passage, 1 Sam xiv. 45, has a servant See Deut xii 18 , Josh. xviii 14 ; 2 Sam iii 8 ; 1 Kings xii 10 ; xviii 21 , 2 Chron x. 10

[4] It is to be remarked, with regard to this explanation, that the laws of poetic modulation do not sanction it, for in poetry two Rbhias appear in immediate proximity

§ 9. CLAUSE OF ZAQEPH.

ANALYSIS.

1. Zaqeph has two signs, the second being the simple Zaqeph and Psiq prefixed, called then Zaqeph Gadhol. The former is the most common; the latter can occur only in *ditione unius vocis,* that is in clauses of a single word, admitting neither servant nor consecution. Zaqeph Qaton can, however, also occur in clauses of a single word, and the rules for placing Zaqeph Gadhol are somewhat subtle (note 5).

2. The servant of Zaqeph is Munach. Bible *passim.* If a pause less than that indicated by the minor occur immediately before Zaqeph, the Munach may attach to itself a Psiq, Ezek. iii. 27, though Codd. differ. [1] If two words are connected in sense with Zaqeph's word, both will assume Munach, though if there be room for it, one Munach may stand on Zaqeph's own word. Compare Gen. iii. 12, with Gen. xxxvi 32.

When Pashta, the minor, must stand logically on the second word, in that case also Zaqeph's word may assume Munach upon itself. This Munach will then stand where a Metheg might otherwise stand, Gen.

---

[1] It seems a variety of this when the word which is connected bears upon it both a Munach and Mercha, Gen. xxviii. 2 and 6. Numbers xvii. 23 In such cases the Mercha, which in some editions is Metheg, can only be intended to keep up the tone and prevent the last syllable from being altogether toneless.

vii. 21, ix. 15; but not generally on the first letter of a word, on which the Metheg must be allowed to remain, Gen xl. 19, though often Metheg is retained even not on the first letter, and pretty often Munach falls on this letter. Gen xxv 9, in some editions הֲחִתִּי. Exod. v. 7; Ex. iv. 26. [2]

3. The minor of Zaqeph is Pashta. Bible *passim.* Sometimes Ythibh is used for minor under the following conditions—*in ditione unius vocis,* without servant or following of any kind, on a monosyllable or dissyllable penacute, having nothing, not even simple sheva, before the tone. Ythibh is always placed before the vowel which it accents, Gen. xxxi. 7; Deut. i. 4. [3] Zaqeph *in ditione unius vocis,* may assume Pashta, its minor, on its own word, under certain restrictions. It cannot stand on the first [4] letter of a word, but may stand on the second or third, provided this syllable be shut, and provided, between this syllable and the place of Zaqeph, there be a syllable, simple or composite sheva, however, sufficing in this case to form a syllable. [5]

---

[2] See Spitzner, sec 171-173

[3] Ythibh, it is evident, is simply Mahpach, the servant of Pashta, with another name and position as well as function; and Ewald acutely conjectures that it was thought enough in the case of the single word to expand the pronunciation of the Mahpach, and elevate it thus into a slight distinctive. That it is a distinctive, appears from Zachar, iv 6 where Dag lene follows it. When Ewald adds that Zaqeph's word does not then willingly assume Munach upon itself, quoting Deut xi 21, as authority, his remark is hardly justified by usage. Exod v 7, 2 Sam i 22, etc. Lehrbuch, p 180, sec 97 m.

[4] But that this is not an unchangeable principle is proved by Gen xix 27. Nordheimer (ii p 337 *b*) is wrong in restricting the position of Pashta to the *second* letter; it may stand also on the first, Gen xix 27, or third, Lev xxii 12. He is also not sufficiently precise when he says that a vowel is requisite between the two accents, seeing a simple moveable sheva is sufficient, Gen xxxiv 12. It will be found that usually a simple sheva precedes the Pashta, but occasionally *vav,* with Shureq, and even a short vowel, Gen xxi 33; sometimes both Shureq and a vowel, Lev xxii 12. Conf Spitzner, p 139-140. Ewald, Lehrbuch, p 181.

[5] Now may be understood the general principle on which Zaqeph Gadhol takes the place of Z. Qaton. Of course it must be *in ditione unius vocis,* and besides this it will generally be on a word of such sort,

4. The major to Zaqeph is Rbhia. Bible *passim*. This major may be repeated four times, but in such cases Pashta will be substituted for one or more of the Rbhias In general, [6] when Rbhia is to be repeated there must be three or more words between the Rbhias; in other terms, a Rbhia succeeded by another Rbhia nearer the beginning of the verse, must have a government of three or more words. When the Rbhia, nearest Zaqeph, presides over a *ditio* of fewer than three words, its place is taken by Pashta, which then seems *repetitus*, Gen. i. 7. But the principle is best seen when the second or third Rbhia has too few words between it and its successor, Gen. ix. 12; Exod. iv. 18. See Spitzner, sec. 167. Ouseel, p. 241 ff. Of course if Pashta take the place of Rbhia, Ythibh, the substitute of Pashta, may also do so under the ordinary conditions of its own appearance.

that neither Metheg, nor Munach, nor Pashta, can be placed upon it, in addition to Zaqeph See the rules in 2 and 3. But this is only a general rule, for it actually occurs where Metheg and Munach might be found, Gen xxvi 26 though, perhaps, not where Pashta could appear The word will generally be short, and thus the accent which is composed in this way of the union of two, will be extended into a kind of circumflex, to indicate which the double sign is employed. Ewald, p 181

[6] The rule is only general, for cases occur where Pashta is found in a ditio of four words or even more, Exod viii 13; Deut iii. 21 These exceptions suggest the question, whether the principle of explanation adopted be correct So far, however, as we have been able to see, Pashta, when governing a *ditio* of more than three words, is not substitutus, but repetitus, that is, will always be found immediately next to a Pashta and not next to a Rbhia Numb. xxii 5, xxvi. 58, 2 Sam ix 7, 1 Kings xiv 21 Luzzatto, in his curious letter appended to Baci's *Torath Emeth*, lays down the rule, that if Zaqeph's clause have *three* divisions, the one next Z will be made by Pash, the one farthest by Rb, and the middle by R if the proper interval (§ 10 note 3) occur between it and the furthest, if not, by Pash If the clause have *four* divisions, the nearest two are Pashtas, the furthest two Rbhias, if the required interval appear; if not, there will be one R and *three* P; but this being unmusical, the middle Pashta will become Rbhia, so that the accents will alternate, pp 64-65.

§ 10. CLAUSE OF TIPPECHA.

ANALYSIS.

1. The servant of Tippecha is Mercha. Bible *passim*. If a slight pause has to be indicated between the servant and Tippecha, the servant may assume a Psiq, Gen. xviii. 15 ; Exod. xxxiv. 23.

2. The Minor of Tippecha is Tbhir. Bible *passim*. This minor may be repeated once. This repetition is most common, perhaps, when the one Tbhir immediately succeeds the other, Gen. viii. 17. It occurs also frequently when a single word intervenes, bearing the servant of Tbhir, Deut. iv. 38; and seldom when more than one word intervenes, Deut. xxvi. 2.[1]

When the clause of Tippecha consists of only two words, besides the word on which itself stands, there happens a crowding together of accents upon the middle word. The clause, if it consist of four words, would appear thus ⌣ ⌣ ⌣ ⌣ Tippecha, servant to Tippecha; minor to Tippecha, servant to minor. But the two clausules run together ; the two middle accents, so to speak, coalesce ; and there appears the following order ⌣ ⌣ ⌣, the double Mercha (Mercha Kphulah) representing the broadened accent, which necessarily results from the combination of the two.[2]

---

[1] Ouseel, chap. 8, sec. 8.

[2] The Masorah on Numbers xxxii. 42, enumerates *fourteen* such cases, in all of which Tippecha's clause consists of *three* words, excepting

3. The major of Tippecha is Rbhia. This Rbhia may bear repetition if necessary, Numb. xxviii. 14. This repetition is only possible, however, owing perhaps to the peculiar sound of Rbhia, when several words intervene between the accents; in other cases a Pashta is substituted for one of the Rbhias, Deut. xxviii. 14; Numb. vii. 87; Gen. xxxviii. 12.[3]

Ezek xiv. 4, where the major of Tippecha is found. It is difficult to say whether Mercha Kphulah be a servant or a minor, it seems partly both For on the one hand and side, the aspirate following does not take Dag lene, Exod v. 15, that is, Mercha Kphulah is a *servant*, and on the other hand and side, the word preceding takes Darga, the servant of Tbhir, that is, Mercha Kphulah appears as a minor disjunctive Darga occurs without exception The instances are—Gen xxvii 25; Ex v. 15; Lev x 1; Numb xiv 3, xxxii 42 1 Kings x. 3, xx 29, Ezek, xiv. 4; Zach iii 2; Hab i. 3, Ezra. vii. 25, Nehem iii 38, 2 Chron. ix. 2; xx. 30 See Spitzner, § 182

[3] Luzzatto, in his letter already alluded to, endeavours to fix the limits of the interchange of R and P more rigidly than had been previously attempted. After a severe cut at *Caspar Ledebuhr*, who made lists of phenomena but drew no conclusion from them, and an unkinder cut at *Wasmuth*, who copied out Ledebuhr's lists, especially the mistakes, and concluded that no conclusion was to be drawn from them, R and P being used indifferently, Luz decides that the use of R succeeded by another R., or of R. succeeded by P is dependent on the interval between the two accents (תלויה במרחק שבין שני הטעמים) More particularly; the number of words that intervene between the two Rbhias must be at least *four*, and these four words must contain at least *eight* vowels If in the four words there be only seven vowels R will not be doubled but Pashta *Conf.* Numb xix 2, with Jerem. xxxviii 12 Further, if there are only *three* words intervening between the words to be marked by Rb., these three words must contain at least *ten* vowels, or if fewer, Rb must give way and Pashta be doubled *Conf* Ezek. iv 13, or Ezek xxxviii 17, with Numb. xxvi 58 Tor Em , p. 63

§ 11. CLAUSE OF RBHIA.

ANALYSIS.

1. The servant of Rbhia is Munach. Bible *passim.* Occasionally the Munach stands on Rbhia's own word, Ex. xxxii. 31. Should the third word be more closely united to the second, than the second to the last, the second still takes Munach and the third Darga. This conjunction is called by Ouseel and others, the minimus, and if it occurs at all, must occupy the second and third words. Another minim is Munach with Psiq, which may stand on the second or third word, and may be repeated or may stand next to the first minim which will stand next to Rbhia; in all which cases of repetition, the minor Geresh will be found.

2. The minor to Rbhia is Geresh or Gereshayin. The latter can stand only on a word with the accent on the final syllable and prefers no consecution, tolerating at most one word in addition to its own, and this second word must have no syllable, not even Sheva, before the tone. This minor may accent on the word immediately next Rbhia's word.[1]

3. The major of Rbhia is Tlisha Gdholah.

---

[1] This minor Geresh, as explained in § 5, often falls out See next

4. Rbhia's maximus is Pazer. Instead of Pazer may be found the union of the Tlishas, called Qarne-pharah, or Great Pazer: should the maximus require repetition, Pazer itself must be used as repetitus, Qarne-pharah not tolerating to be repeated. See table and explanation, No. 8.[2]

[2] Luzzatto in his letter to Baer (Tor. Em., pp 54–71) endeavours to find some of the principles regulating the use of the minor, major, etc of Rbhia, etc. He repeats (what he had already said in his *Prolegomeni*) his belief that there are only *ten* distinctive prose accents. Tlish Gdb and Pazer have no independent power or place of their own, but are mere sub-stitutes for Geresh. The following are some of the principles regulating their use —

(1) Two Ger. cannot come together or be used in succession unless an accent of greater power intervene; in other cases, the Ger. nearest the beginning of the verse becomes Tlish Gdhol

(2) Also Tlish. Gd cannot be repeated immediately; if, then, Ger. should occur *three* times, the initial one will become Pazer, leaving the middle one Tlish Gd as before

(3) Tlish Gd cannot come immediately next Tlish Qt , in this posi-tion it becomes again Pazer (p 61)

(4) Also if Geresh fall out but its servant Qadma remain, another Ger. nearer the beginning will often become Tlish Gd.

(5) Geresh is often changed to Tlish Gdhol. if the word on which it stands be small

(6) Although it is generally the Ger nearest the beginning that becomes changed to Tl. Gd , occasionally this remains, and the Ger nearest the verse-end becomes Tlish , p 62 See his Grammatica della Lingua Ebraica, p. 48 and p 55, etc

§ 12. CLAUSES OF TBHIR, ZARQA, AND PASHTA.

ANALYSIS.

1. The ordinary servant of Tbhir is Darga; of Zarqa, Munach; and of Pashta, Mahpach.

2. The common extraordinary servant of all is Mercha, which serves Tbhir when between the tone-syllable of Tbhir's word and the tone-syllable of the servant's word there do not intervene two syllables; Sheva and Pattach furtive being allowed, however, to constitute a syllable.

The same Mercha is servant to Zarqa, as remarked by the Masorah on Ex. vi. 6, in *eleven* cases, though under what conditions is not easily discoverable.

Mercha likewise assumes the place of Mahpach as servant to Pashta, when between the tone-syllables of the two words there does not intervene a syllable, though Pattach furtive and Sheva are allowed to pass as a syllable.

Should a distinction slighter than that indicated by the minor be wanted before any of these three distinctives, a minimus is formed out of their respective servants, ordinary or extraordinary, with or without Psiq.

3. The common minor to these accents as to Rbhia is Geresh or Gereshayim, the latter under the same restrictions as in Rbhia's clause. This minor may occupy the word next the distinctive, though not usually,

and generally only when the word of Rbhia is long or compound.

As explained under the general table (section 5) the Geresh in the clauses of Rbhia, Tbhir, Zarqa and Pashta may fall out, and the two clauses slide into each other, in which case the *servants* of these four accents assume the functions of Geresh, and act as distinctives. Qadma still continuing its former duty of servant.

4. The ordinary major to these three accents as to Rbhia is Tlisha Gdholah. In a certain number of cases the minor and major are found transposed. This transposition, though taking place under Tbhir, Zarqa, and Pashta, does not appear under Rbhia. See Gen. xiii. 1; Is. ix. 5; Nehem. iii. 15. The transposition is not of common occurrence.[1]

The maximus to Tbhir, Zarqa, and Pashta is Pazer, as in the case of Rbhia. Instead of the Pazer, the double Tlisha Qarne-pharah may occur. In the case of Zarqa, Ezek. xlviii. 21; 2 Chron. xxxv. 7; in the case of Pasha, Josh. xix. 51, etc.; in the case of Tbhir, Jer. xxxvii. 25.[2]

[1] See note 2 in § 11, from Luzzatto.
[2] See the cases discussed by Ouseel under these accents respectively.

§ 13. CLAUSES OF GERESH, PAZER, ETC.

ANALYSIS.

1. The governments of these accents have been discussed with all necessary fulness in § 5 under the general table. The servant of Geresh is Qadma, but with monosyllables or penacutes, it is Munach if in a clause of two words, but if in a greater clause it is still Qadma. If a third word be taken into the society of these, it is accented by Tlisha Qtannah, and all following words by Munach, any of which may have Psiq attached. Very rarely Munach with Psiq stands next to Qadma without Tlisha Qtannah, Is. iv. 19. Occasionally Qadma will appear on the same word with Geresh, Exod. v. 10.

2. Pazer places Munach on every word between itself and the beginning of the verse, to which Psiq may be added if a small distinction require to be indicated, but if a great distinction occur, Pazer will be repeated with the same following as before. Instead of Pazer, Qarne-pharah occurs eleven times, which must have on the word next it (and it requires a government of several words), Yerach ben Yomo, but all succeeding words will assume Munach.

3. Tlisha Gdholah, like Pazer, imposes Munach on every word in its clause, to any of which Psiq may be added, if necessary.

THE

POETIC ACCENTUATION

AS EXHIBITED IN THE

PSALMS, PROVERBS, AND JOB.

עִקָּר גָּדוֹל הוּא לִשְׁמֹר דֶּרֶךְ הַטְּעָמִים

ABEN EZRA.

POETIC ACCENTUATION.

§ 1.

The same principles are to be observed in the poetic as in the prosaic accents. There is a certain order in which disjunctives are found. Counting from the end or place of Silluq, the ordinary distinctive next to Silluq is called its minor, because its distinctive power relatively to Silluq is of course much less than the distinctive power of an accent nearer the beginning of the verse. Some prefer to call these distinctives Elevations (of the voice). It is a question of name: the elevation is greater the further from the end. The ordinary distinctive between this one and the beginning of the stanza, if it stands in immediate logical relation to Silluq (and not in immediate logical subordination to this *minor*) will be greater in power than the first, and may be called Silluq's major; the third will be its maximus. The same law will apply to any other distinctive taken as the base or final accent of a clause: it may have a number of distinctives all successively and immediately related to it, which will increase in distinctive power the further they are removed from it towards the beginning of the verse, and will be named its minor, major, maximus, etc. These are names which are useful to indicate the position and order of the distinctives and express the logical principle of the accentuation; the term elevations or risings, with its opposite, sinkings or fallings, expresses rather the other or rhythmical principle. What is called a minimus is an extraordinary distinctive of less power than the minor, and has its rise in the principle that of three words which are all connected together, some two must stand nearer to each other than any of them does to the third, *e.g.*, 1. 2. 3, will be 1–(2. 3) or (1. 2)–3 of necessity. If, then, this distinction be too little for the accent called the minor, this less distinction will be indicated by a sign designated the minimus, which is often a servant or connective with Psiq, or some other combination of servants. This kind of pause is in very many cases not logical at all, but purely oratorical and a Begadh-kephath letter coming after it, will not always assume Dagesh. In the Psalms, the use of these slight pauses is an exceedingly intricate matter, and apparently incapable of being reduced to rule from the almost endless diversity presented by MSS. and Edd. In these exquisite Lyrics the rise and fall and flow of feeling is much more diverse than in ordinary prose composition; and the accentual system, like the vowel system, being a true phonography— all these infinitely varied feelings expressed in proper corresponding human tones, to the minutest shade of joy or pain, and made sensible to the eye—we may expect a system of points having some relation in intricacy and diversity to the inextricable complexity of the feelings of the human heart and the unexampled capacity of the human voice to give them utterance. We shall never, perhaps, find the key to this perplexed labyrinth till we can discover something like the vocal values of the separate accents. This we have little means of knowing, the present Jewish reading being quite unreliable; but there cannot be room to doubt that the punctuators proceeded on a plan, and on certain recognised values or tones expressed by particular symbols, and that all this confused heaping of small accents together is not without a meaning, but bears within it a language which could we read it we should find natural, and beautiful because natural. At the same

time our failure in this point does not entail any very
serious consequences; we are pretty well able still to
eliminate the logical significance of the accents, and this
concerns us chiefly. The reasons for placing this or that
particular small disjunctive or connective rather than
another need not be very minutely investigated by those
whose aim is purely hermeneutical, for these reasons will
be found to depend chiefly on musical considerations,
and to vary according to the subjective feeling of the
punctuator, the remarkable diversity in MSS. and Edd.
making it quite evident that complete harmony had
never been attained among the authors of the system;
making it evident, indeed, that the system is not at all
the result of concert, but the gradual growth of perhaps
several centuries. And hence it requires no very pro-
found study to discover the futility of the rules laid down
by Ouseel and even Spitzner for the use of extraordinary
servants or consecutions. Ouseel proceeds upon .the
assumption that if an unusual accent makes its appear-
ance the reason must be exclusively in the prosody of
the immediate passage—its long or short words, the
number of its words, the place of accent on the word,
the word as dageshed or undageshed, and such super-
ficial considerations. But however much may be due
to these circumstances, they are by no means sufficient
to account for the phenomena, for the rules laid down
by this prosodian are often violated with the unanimous
concurrence of editions. We must take into considera-
tion another more general and deeper law than the
relation of mere syllables, namely, the feeling which the
reader associated with the passage, which he expressed
by his voice, and which the accentuation sought to ex-
press by symbols. This feeling, or, at least, the vocal
expression of it, might in most cases be traditional; the
reader knew not why he read so; he had learned it, his
fathers had learned it, and the accentuator perpetuated
it; and because feeling is unspeakably diverse, and in-
capable of being confined by laws, the accentual signs

symbolizing it will partake of its wildness and licence.
And tradition too of necessity, when but a tradition of
tones, was imperfect and fluctuating, and this fluctuation
has been added to by the unavoidable mistakes and sub-
stitutions of frequent transcription. But it is this deep,
ever-varying fountain of feeling bursting up in a thou-
sand forms, and running in streams of a thousand diffe-
rent colors, hardly ever the same in any two Psalms,
which can roll in full volume and unimpeded through
the channel of human utterance, but finds itself confined
and cramped within the bounds of ordinary accentual
law, and thus overflows and cuts for itself a new bed,—
it is this that accounts for such endless diversity of
punctuation in the poetic books, and makes any funda-
mental investigation into the poetic accents a task so
difficult and in many cases of so little importance.
Obviously, if we are to be thorough, we must proceed
by endeavouring first of all to ascertain the vocal value
of the various separate accents, and with this as a key
advance to the opening up of their combinations. But,
unfortunately, it is only from their combinations that
we can learn their individual values, and thus our in-
vestigation moves in an almost hopeless circle. We
must know the meaning of the separate accents to un-
derstand an accented poem; and we have only before us
accented poems whence to discover the meaning of the
separate accents. In such a position it is only the most
general principles that we can arrive at, only the laws,
which are not very profound, and which a moderate skill
in physiology can detect: deep down there may be
unfelt currents running, and elusive connections esta-
blished, and subtle influences reaching through the en-
tire mechanism of the system, which we cannot discover
or even suspect. But nevertheless the more familiar we
are with outward laws, the more likely are we to leap
from without to what is inner and deeper; and by know-
ing well the surface where the nervous filaments take
their rise, we shall gradually work our way deeper till

we reach at last the inmost heart and life : and the fuller
our understanding of the system becomes, the fuller will
be our admiration of the singular humanity as well as
singular ingenuity of the men whose reverence urged
them to set such a hedge about their Scriptures that not
only no letter but no tone of a letter should be lost.

There is not much in the poetic accents differing in
form from those in prose. The place of Sgolta is as-
sumed in appearance by ⌐⌐ Mercha Mahpach, a com-
pound accent, and therefore implying a double or rising
and falling inflection. In reality, however, Mercha
Mahpach represents in poetry the place held by Athnach
in prose. The prose and poetic verse, while agreeing in
this, that both fall asunder into two chief sections, and
in this, that one of these sections is again sub-divided
into two, so that the verse in both seems to contain *three*
divisions, yet differ in this, that in prose it is the initial
section that is sub-divided, and in poetry the concluding
section. Thus—

$$: \overline{} \cdots\cdots \; \| \overline{} \cdots\cdots\cdots \cdots | \overline{} \cdots \}$$

$$: \overline{} \cdots\cdots \; | \overline{} \cdots\cdots\cdots \cdots \| \overline{} \cdots \}$$

Similar to Mercha Mahpach is the accent ⌐, Rbhia
Mugrash (Gereshed R.), which stands related to Silluq
in poetry as Tippecha does in prose; it is a double or
broadened Rbhia, logically of the same value as the
simple Rbhia with which it is often interchanged, and
differing solely in its rhythmical or inflectional signifi-
cance. The number of compound accents is greater in
poetry than in prose, which was to be anticipated from
the nearer approach to music made by the poetic accents
and the necessary crowding together of tones on the
same word, occasionally even on the same syllable.
The poetic symbols are as follows :—

DISJUNCTIVES	CONNECTIVES
: ⌐ Silluq with Soph Pasuq.	⌐ Mercha (occasionally Munach)

DISJUNCTIVES		CONNECTIVES
֭ Mercha Mahpach [1]	.	֗ Yerach ben Yomo.[2]
֘ Athach	.	֤ Munach [3] (occasionally Mercha).
— Rbhia	.	Mercha or Mahpach.
֮ R. Mugrash [4] . .	.	Mercha.
֖ Tippecha Anterior [5]	.	Munach.
֮ Zarqa [6]	.	Munach (and Mercha).
֓ Pazer . .	.	Yerach or Galgal.
֡ Shalsheleth with Psiq	.	No servant or sec. except in three cases.
֝ } Azla Legarmeh [7] . .	.	֤ Mahpach.
֝ } Mahpach Legarmeh	.	No servant or secution.
		֧ Mercha Zarqatum.[8]
		֧ Mahpach with Zarqa
		֖ Tippecha non anterior.[9]
		֬ Munach Superior.
		֒ Shalsheleth without
		֨ Azla (Qadma). [Psiq.

The accent Zinnorith may be distinguished from Zinnor by its function and position. As to function, it is a servant, or, as Michaelis names it, " conservus," appear-

---

[1] Called generally by the poetic accentuists עוֹלֶה וְיוֹרֵד, *going up and coming down*, either from its tone or the position of the symbol (Baer) Mercha in like manner is named יוֹרֵד because its sound is a falling tone

[2] Called גַּלְגַּל *wheel*, sometimes אוֹפָן, the same.

[3] Called by Ben Asher כִּי קוֹלוֹ לְמַעֲלָה יָרוּם - עוֹלָה   Tor Emeth, p 5. All these connectives appear as already noticed (p. 31) with the title שׁוֹפַר ר'מְגָרָשׁ, i e R Gereshed

[5] Called by the native accentuists *dechi* דחי, i e *push*, thrust; either from its peculiar tone or because it stands away from the place of the tone. On account of its position it is called יְמָנִית, because standing at the *right* of the word. It appears always before the first vowel of the word.

[6] Zarqa is generally called צָנוֹר in poetic accentuation. Both names mean *spout*

[7] That is *per se* לְגַרְמֵהּ.

[8] Zarqa, when used as a " conservus," is commonly called Zinnorith.

[9] Usually called Tarcha טַרְחָא.

ing along with the servants Mercha and Mahpach on the same word; and, as to position, on the open syllable before the tone, or sometimes on a small independent word, being an open monosyllable. Zinnor again is a distinctive, and stands on the last letter of its word.

The accents Tippecha anterior and non-anterior are equally distinguished by function and position. Tippecha anterior is a disjunctive and appears always on the right of its word immediately before the first vowel, so that it falls completely outside the word. Tippecha non-anterior or Tarcha is a conjunctive, and stands on the place of accent.

Munach occasionally assumes its position above the word[10] (M. superior): this indicates that though a connective or depression, its connecting power is almost gone, and that it rises nearly to the elevation of a disjunctive.

Shalsheleth occurs only *eight* times according to the Masorah without Psiq. Without Psiq it is a connective, though it is to be observed that it is not an ordinary servant; it never stands immediately next to a disjunctive, but always with one or more servants intervening. With Psiq it is a disjunctive occurring chiefly in the clause of Silluq. and being in all cases except Job xi. 6, immediately taken up by Athnach.[11]

It has been fully established by Baer, the author of Torath Emeth, that Qadma Psiq or Azla Legarmeh, and Mahpach Psiq or Mahpach Legarmeh, are the same accent logically, and that the laws for regulating the use of the one or the other are purely prosodial or musical. The former is always employed when there are more words in connection, the latter when standing alone and when the accent is on the first syllable.

---

[10] Called then עֹלֶ֜ה Illui   Ben Asher names it תולה, *suspending.* Tor Emeth, p. 5

[11] Ewald puts Shalsheleth among the connectives expressly, Lehrb, p. 191, although he makes it play the part of a distinctive, p 194, 2, and p 197, 3, where he names it *Stellvertreter* of R Mugrash. He disregards the Masoretic distinction of Shal. Psiq and without Psiq

From the more regular form of verse than prose, and the nicer balance of the members of the stanza, it will follow that the various clauses will be in general much shorter than in prose, and more equable in their length ; there will be much less of subordination of one clause to another than in logical narrative, and hence far fewer sub-clauses, which are rare in poetry, hardly going beyond one in each of the great divisions of the verse. There will, therefore, hardly ever occur a repetition of the same distinctive accent. The only three that bear repetition are Rbhia, Zinnor, and Legarmeh, and even these to a small extent.

§ 2. INTERPUNCTION.

A verse may have one, two, or three clauses, as in prose. The verse always ends with Silluq as there. If there be three sections, the middle one will be made by Athnach, and the greatest by Olehveyored. If there occur but two sections, the second may be made either by Athnach or Olehveyored, the former having a less distinctive power in poetry than the other. The position and powers of the chief distinctives are seen from the following scheme :—

	1	2	3	4	5	6	7	etc.
(a) :	⸽	(serv.)	⸻	⸻	⸻	⸻	⸻	etc.
(b) :	⸽	⸻	⸻	⸻	⸻	⸻	⸻	etc.

1. The first line (a) represents the usual positions of the metrical distinctives, the second line (b) their positions in extraordinary circumstances. The ordinary place of Olehveyored is on the sixth, seventh, etc. word from the verse-end, on any of which it may appear provided that word be not the first in the verse, in which case Legarmeh takes its place.[1] Olehveyored may stand however on the fifth, though not nearer the end. It rests there of necessity when Athnach is also required by the sense on the fourth or third word ; in other circumstances it will indicate a superior emphasis to that of Athnach.

2. The ordinary position of Athnach is the fourth or fifth word from the end, but it may shift a place either way, having thus the choice of four places. It will always be on the fifth if a great distinctive be required

---

[1] Baer in Delitzsch, s. 504.

on that word, when R. Mug. or Shalsheleth must also
be on the fourth. It will also be on the fifth when R.
Mug. is on the second and accompanied by two ser-
vants, or when Silluq has three servants. In extraor-
dinary circumstances it will ascend to the sixth; for
example, when Silluq has four servants, Ps. xxxii. 5,[2]
(though not in Ps. iii, 3), and sometimes when R. Mug.
must be on the third word with two servants, or on the
second with three. In two cases, Job xxxii. 6, Ps.
xviii. 1, Athnach reaches the seventh and *eighth* words
respectively. Athnach may descend to the third, though
not lower. It will be there of necessity when the sense
demands R. Mug. on the second and a strong distinctive
on the third; sometimes emphasis will require Athnach
ou the third when the second has a servant, provided the
servant's word be long with two full syllables or one
open syllable and Sheva before the tone.[3] Athnach,
however, cannot stand on the first word of a verse, but
is there represented by Pazer.[4]

3. The ordinary place of R. Mugrash is the third
word, but it may ascend to the fourth when a distinctive
is required on the third, and in a few instances when
Silluq has two servants, though in that case Shalsheleth
Psiq regularly represents R. Mug. on the fourth word.[5]
R. Mug. descends to the second when the sense demands
it, provided Silluq's word be long, that is, have two
syllables or one open syllable, and Sheva before the
tone.[6]

---

[2] Ouseel, p 34.   [3] Ibid, p. 30   [4] Baer in Delitzsch, s. 506
          [5] Ouseel, p 29   [6] Ibid, p 26

§ 3. METRICAL TABLE.

The following table embodies the principal elements of the metrical system :—

ANALYSIS

1. Silluq stands at the end by itself, and forms, as the base of all, a class with which none of the other accents is to be compared.[1] The lines marked I. II. etc. are disjunctives, the intermediate lines their respective connectives.

2. II. gives the *minors* of the *opposite* accents in I., and the last accent in II. is the maximus of I.

3. III. gives the minors of the opposite accents in II., and the last accent in III. is the maximus of all those in II.

4. III. has a common consecution ; minor, Legarmeh ; major, Pazer, with its servant Galgal ; the minor of Pazer is also Legarmeh. Whenever Legarmeh has a servant, of necessity Azla Legarmeh is to be used. This consecution is properly that of Rbhia, but is common to it with Dechi and Zinnor.[2]

---

[1] Spitzner also places Silluq by itself as unlike all the other accents.

[2] This full consecution of Rbhia may be seen, Ps cvi. 48. Ewald makes Zinnor perform the duty which is here assigned to Rbhia as max. of R. Mugrash But, in the first place, his view destroys the unity attained by making Rbhia great distinctive to the three accents standing immedi-

5. A few more general facts suffice to give almost an exhaustive view of the metrical system.

(*a*) :— — becomes :— — when the servant's word is monosyllabic or penacute; and if there be two words connected together immediately before Silluq, thus, 1 – (2.3), the pointing is :— — —, an exceeding common combination.[3]

(*b*) — — becomes — — when there are only *two* words in the clause, or when an accent greater than Dechi immediately follows, but not with Dechi itself. As in (*a*) the relation of three words may be 1 – (2.3), which assumes the exceedingly common form — — —.

(*c*) — — becomes — — when there are only two words in the clause, or when there are more words if the distinction must fall on the second word.

(*d*) — — becomes — — when the servant's word is monosyllabic or penacute or has Dagesh *forte* or *lene* in the accented consonant.

(*e*) — — is — — in many cases, especially when the accent falls on the first or second letter.

(*f*) The accents Mercha and Mahpach may in all cases assume Zinnorith as a helping servant, provided there be one or more open syllables before the tone-syllable, on which Zinnorith can stand.[4]

(*g*) The accent Mahpach is a very common variant for almost any servant, and its use as second or third servant is of very frequent occurrence.

(*h*) It often happens, so often as to constitute a rule, that the minor to a weak accent may become the minim to an accent of greater power; thus Legarmeh, the minor of III., serves as a very small distinctive to I. and II.

---

ately related to Silluq; and, in the second place, Rbhia occurs under R. Mug. much more frequently than Zinnor, the latter being the well known substitute of Rbhia both in poetry and prose.

[3] Tippecha in this connection is not anterior, but stands on the place of tone, and is thus easily distinguished from Dechi the disjunctive.

[4] Baer says, Tor. Em., p. 9, that Zinnorith has in these cases no note of its own; but this view is sufficiently refuted by Luzzatto in his letter appended to Baer's Tractate, p. 55–6.

(ι) Very often is to be found in Edd. of the Bible, Rbhia simple, where the analogy of the table would lead to expect R. Mugrash, and in some Edd., *e.g.* Hahn, even conversely. The latter is, doubtless, a blunder; the former occurs chiefly in short sentences, such as the titles of the Psalms, and is to be explained, not on logical but on rhythmical principles. (See § of R. Mug.) For more particular information the following sections must be consulted.

§ 4. CLAUSE OF SILLUQ.

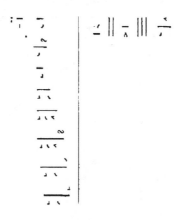

ANALYSIS.

1. The ordinary servant of Silluq, as in prose, is Mercha. This Mercha may assume Tsinnorith upon its own word, if there be an open syllable before the place of accent, v. 7. Tsinnorith may stand even on an independent word if that word be an open monosyllable, and Mercha be retracted to the first syllable of its own word, xviii. 20.[1] According to the Masorah, in Tor. Em., p. 13, after B. B., p. 7, three passages, lxix. 15 ; civ. 6 ; Job, xii. 15, are pointed with Tippecha on the servant's word. It is probable that Munach has fallen out (2). If the word of the servant be monosyllabic or penacute, the servant of Silluq is Munach, B. B. p. 7 ; iii. 7 ; iv. 5 ; v. 2, etc. This substitution is occasioned by the peculiarity of Mercha's tone, which, according

[1] Tor. Em., p. 9

to Ben Asher, has a low expanded note.[2] Edd. often write Munach where no such reason can be assigned, *e.g.* Hahn, Job vi. 3 ; vi. 7 ; vi. 8, etc., and not unfrequently refuse to write it when such reason demands it Hahn, Job vii. 16.

2. If two words are to be connected pretty closely with the word of Silluq, but have for each other a closer affinity than the second has for Silluq's word, thus. 1- (2. 3), then, as already detailed (§ 3), the double accent ⎯⏑ arises ; Munach being an actual though exceeding slight disjunctive, so slight as often not to admit Daghesh on the immediately succeeding aspirate, and Tippecha being a real though slight connective, not usually[3] admitting Dag. ; Prov. i. 13, and often.

It will not unfrequently happen that both these accents stand on the same word, Ps. xlv. 15, if a Metheg might otherwise have stood.[4]

3. When three words stand in connection with Silluq's word, then the two already pointed remain as in (2), and the third assumes Mahpach if the accent be on the first syllable of the word, xxiv. 10, xxxix. 12, Job. xiv. 13 ; if the accent be on the second syllable, and the first

[2] Hence he calls this servant יוֹרֵד, Tor Em., p 5. So Ben Bilam, p iv.

[3] The fact seems to be that the relation of the three words may be 1- (2. 3), or (1 2) -3 , in the former case Mun. would be followed by Dag but Tippecha not , in the latter, Mun. would not have Dag but Tippecha would. B B excepts from this rule the passage cix 16, which he points with Illui as first serv and Tipp (Tarcha) as second Baer, on the contrary, Illui as first and Azla as second. Mich., Hahn, etc., point regularly.

[4] According to Tor. Emeth, p. 11, this double accent can appear on one word only when R. Mug is not to follow. Should this accent follow, then the word will assume the usual Mercha, and retain its Metheg. Edd *e g*. Theile, write Metheg and Munach, thus introducing intolerable confusion, ii. 5 The author of Tor Em lays down the further rule that if the accents come together, from the word next Silluq being penacute, the form is ⎯⏑. He points his own Psalter so, *e g* v. 11, but Edd do not agree with him. Mich uses Maqqeph. The small inscriptions of *eight* Psalms instead of Munach and Mercha take two Munachs superior, Ps. xxxvi, xliv, xlvii, xlix., lxi., lxix , lxxxi., lxxxv. See the Masorah, quoted Tor Em., p. 13.

an open syllable, the Mahpach will assume Zinnorith on the open vowel, xxviii. 8.

But if the accent fall on the second syllable and the first be not open, or if it fall on any syllable nearer the word-end, then Azla is employed, Ps. xlii. 2, an example which shows that Azla is here a servant and not a disjunctive, with Psiq fallen out, as Ouseel (p. 65) supposes, for no Dag. follows in the next word.

This rule is in conformity with Ben Asher's pointing, but Ben Naphtali puts Mahpach on the second syllable, xliii. 1, and Edd. Job xxii. 12, Prov. xxix. 13; and, indeed, there is not one of the above rules but Edd. frequently contradict. Thus Theile and Mich. write Azla on the first letter, liv. 5; so they write Azla on the second syllable with an open syllable preceding, lxxxiv. 9, lxi. 5, lix. 6. Sometimes, instead of Azla on the fourth word, Munach superior appears, iv. 8, though under what conditions is not very obvious.[5] B. Bil.'s rule is simple. If the accent be on first letter, it is Mahpach; if on the second, Illui; if on the third, etc., Azla, p. 8. Passages where more than three servants occur are ni. 3, of which the usual pointing is $\stackrel{\llcorner}{}\ \stackrel{\llcorner}{}\ \stackrel{\llcorner}{}$ but Baer points with the ordinary Munach Tippechatum; xxxii. 5, xlii. 2. As to the passage cxxv. 3, see clause of Legarmeh.

4. The ordinary minor to Silluq is R. Mugrash; the major, Athnach; the maximus, Olehveyored. Several peculiarities, however, have to be noticed with regard to the interpunction of Silluq's clause. The following scheme shows the most important:

---

[5] Baer, Delitzsch, ii., p. 487, would write Mun. sup always when $\stackrel{\vee}{\underline{}}$ would otherwise appear, were not the open syllable formed by one of the letters ובכלם, on which Zinnorith cannot stand. Baer, of course, points his own Psalter in conformity with this rule. Not so Michaelis. See his note, Ps iv 8, and his punctuation of lxxvi. 4, lxxviii. 25, cxix. 84 See Ew. Lehrb. 197.

(a) [accent diagram]

(b) [accent diagram]

(c) [accent diagram]

(d) [accent diagram]

(*a*) This line presents the most usual appearance of the interpunction, the division falling at the third word, and made by R. Mug. The servant of Silluq will be on the second, and vary according to the rules in (1). R. Mug. may be taken up immediately by the major, or it may be followed by one or more servants. If the division fall on the third word, and no more divisions be required in the clause of Silluq (i.e. *before* the occurrence of the major or maximus), the division must be made by R. Mugrash. If more divisions occur the case is that of (*c*).

(*b*) If the division fall on the second word, various cases occur. If there be another distinction in the clause the case is that of (*d*). If there be no more distinctions to be marked in the clause proper of Silluq, either R. Mug. or Munach may stand on the second word, the last, of course, only if Tippecha can follow on the third, or the word be such that Tippecha and Munach can both stand upon one word, xxxi. 17. R. Mug. cannot appear on the second word unless Silluq's word be long, that is, have two syllables, or one open syllable and moveable Sheva before the tone, ii. 1, ii. 2, ii. 6, ii. 8, v. 10. If these conditions be not satisfied, Munach with Tippecha will take the place of R. Mug., iv. 3. This double accent requiring two words, or one word as described in (2), cannot itself appear generally when the major is on the third word. In that case R. Mug. must be present, or, if its conditions are not satisfied, a servant

must take its place. When the division on the second
word is made by R. Mug. or by Munach with Tippecha,
Athnach may follow immediately, or these acccents may
take their servants, v. 4, v. 8, iv. 6, vi. 4.

(c) When two distinctions require to be made in the
clause proper of Silluq, two cases also occur. If the
distinction be on the *third* and *fourth* words, then the
interpunction is as in (c), R. Mug. on the *fourth*,
Legarmeh (always Mahpach Legarmeh) on the *third*,
and Illui on the *second*, iii. 1, x. 14. This form is very
common, and the positions of the accents are invariable.
R. Mug. may then be immediately followed by the
major, taking no servant, xviii. 7, xix. 5, xx. 2; or
having a servant, xviii. 31, xcix. 4. Instead of Mahpach
Legarmeh, Azla Legarmeh occurs once, cxxv. 3, because
there Legarmeh attaches to itself a servant which Mahp.
Leg. cannot do. This passage is also irregular in hav-
ing, according to some Edd., Shalshcleth, according to
others Pazer, instead of R. Mugrash.

(d) If two distinctions have to be made, and they fall
the one at the *second* word and the other at the *fourth*,
the form assumed is that of (d), where the accents and
the positions are again invariable, vii. 6, x. 2, xii. 8,
xiii. 2, xiii. 3, xx. 8, xxix. 11, xxxiii. 12, etc. Shal-
sheleth has always Psiq in this position; it occurs always
in this position except nine times, once with Psiq in the
clause of R. Mugrash, Job xi. 6, and the other eight
times without Psiq as servant; and is always followed
by Athnach, and has no servant with three exceptions.
In one of these exceptional cases, lxxxix. 2, it has *one*
servant, viz., Mercha; in the others it has *two* servants,
Mercha and Tippecha, Job. xxxii. 6, Job xxxvii. 12.[6]
Ben. Bil. gives only the passages in Job.

4. Shalsheleth forms a note which the voice cannot

---

[6] Tor. Emeth, p. 36. As to the Masorah on Shalsheleth, see the note
of Michaelis, Heb Bible, Ps xiii. 3. R. Mug. occurs, according to Baer,
twice for Shal in (d), xlvi. 8, xlvi. 12; but Edd. give many more cases,
iii. 5, lxvi. 3, lxxv. 4, lvi. 3, etc.

immediately start, and hence is not found at the commencement of a verse. On the first word of a verse it will usually be represented by Pazer, xviii. 2, xxx. 1.

In the *eight* cases alluded to by the Masorah, Shalsheleth occurs without Psiq, and is not a disjunctive, but one of the secondary connectives. It cannot stand in the place of an ordinary servant, next a great distinctive, but always appears with at least one other servant intervening between it and the distinctive. In this respect it agrees with Azla.[7] This peculiarity as to position arises from its singular tone, as a thrilling, quivering shake of the voice, a note well represented by its shape.[8]

The passages where Shalsh. occurs as servant are the following :—Ps. iii. 3, in the clause of Silluq ; xxxiv. 8, lxviii. 15, cxxxvii. 9, in the clause of R. Mugrash ; lxv. 2, lxxii. 3, Prov. i. 9, Prov. vi. 27, in the clause of Athnach. In all these passages Shalsheleth attaches another word to its own, and the servant it makes use of is Mahpach; in one passage, lxv. 2, it has two servants, the first Illui, and the second Mahpach.[9]

It is needless to expect editors to conform to a rule which they did not know. Theile puts a Psiq, lxviii. 15, cxxxvii 9, lxv. 2, lxxii. 3 ; so Hahn. lxv. 2, lxviii. 15, etc., though it is not worth while enumerating what such editors put. It is to be expected that their critical taste and tact will refuse to put the Psiq where it ought to be, *e.g.* Theile x. 2, without Psiq.[10]

---

[7] Ewald, Lehrbuch, s. 193-194.

[8] Delitzsch, ii., s. 524, hence the names מרעיד, מרעים, etc.

[9] Torath Emeth, p. 36 It is illustrative of the difficulty of being consistent and accurate in accentuation to notice that Baer in Tor. Em and in his Psalter uses Illui in this example, but in Dehtzsch, p 490, he points the passage with Azla for Illui These passages are also discussed, Ben Bilam, p. 2-3, by whom Shal. is recognised as servant See Hupf Commentatio, part ii., p. 4.

[10] It is more likely to be from obstinacy than ignorance when Ewald writes lxxii 3 with Psiq

Secution of Shalsheleth as distinctive and servant.
(B. B., p. 2–3).

usual position as distinctive,

(once), lxxxix, 3

(twice). Job, xxxii 6, Job, xxxvii, 12

(seven times). See above,

(once), lxv, 2

§ 5. CLAUSE OF RBHIA MUGRASH.

ANALYSIS

1. The ordinary servant of R. Mug. is Mercha, i. 4. This, in favourable circumstances, may assume, in addition, Zarqa, ı. 1, ı. 2, etc,[1]

2. When two words are connected together, the first assumes Mercha, and the second Tippecha, xiv. 1, xix. 8, xix. 9, xxiv. 5, xxiv. 6.[2]

3. When three words are connected pretty closely with the word of R. Mug., the two next R. will remain as in (2), and the third will receive Mahpach, lxxiii. 1; this Mahpach may, in the favourable circumstances, receive Zinnorith, cxix. 25. One passage, xviii. 1, presents extraordinary confusion.

בַּיּוֹם ׀ הִצִּיל־יְיָ אֹתוֹ מִכַּף כָּל־אֹיְבָיו

is the pointing adopted by Baer in his Psalter, with *three* Merchas, and Legarmeh. Curiously enough, in Tor. Em., p. 15, he unites מכף to the next word by Maqqeph, and thus exhibits but two Merchas. The com-

---

[1] Tor Em , p 14. Ben Bilam, p. 3.

[2] Tor. Em ut sup Ben Bilam, p 3. The generally received rule is, that if Athnach do not follow, the above is the form of accent; but if

mon Edd. are altogether unintelligible on this verse,[3]
For the passages xxxiv. 8, lxviii. 15, cxxxvii. 9, where
Shalsheleth occurs, see § iv. 4.

4. The minor of R. Mug. is Dechi. When Dechi
follows R. Mug. there cannot be more than a single
word between them.[4] This minor never appears when
Athnach is to follow; and if it stand next the word of
R. Mugrash, Dechi's word must be long, *i.e.* have two
syllables, or one open syllable and moveable Sheva be-
fore the tone, iv. 5, vi. 1.[5]

5. The minor of R. Mug. is Rbhia simple, which does
not occur, however, if Athnach is to follow,[6] xxxi. 23,
xlix. 15, lvii, 9, etc. It is decidedly against facts when
Ewald maintains that the sub-division in the clause of
R. Mugrash is made by Zinnor.[7]

Very rarely Legarmeh may appear as a very small
distinctive in the clause of Rbhia, cix. 28, occasionally
also when Athnach cannot appear, being requisite on the
first word of a verse, Pazer will take its place.

Note.—It is very common to find simple Rbhia in the
clause of Silluq instead of R. Mugrash. Several scholars,
such as Ouseel, Spitzner, and, according to the latter,
also Wasmuth, believe that when R. Simple occurs for
R. Mugrash, it is merely by omission of the Geresh,
which omission is due to the carelessness of printers or

Athnach follow, both the servants are Merchas With this rule Edd *e g*
Theile, will be found most to agree, though B B expressly contradicts it,
p 3.

[3] Ben Bilam points הַצִּיל with Zarqa, but calls it a servant, the passage
being one where R Mug. has four servants, p 1.

[4] Tor Em , p 15. [5] Ouseel, p 61

[6] Ouseel, p 62 , although it may occur with Olchveyored, xviii 51

[7] Lehrbuch, p 197, 3 Ewald comes to this conclusion on the ground
of the three passages, xviii 1, xxxi 22, lxvi 20. But, even were Edd
and Codd unanimous in giving Zinnor in these passages, they could not, in
opposition to a much larger number of instances, where Rbhia subdivides,
form any ground for a general rule, and much less can they do so when
there is no agreement regarding them among Edd Mich , Ps. xviii. 1,
note, conjectures that Zinnor here and in the other passages was really not
the distinctive, but Zinnorith the "conservus," and proposed a punctuation
which relieved the passages of some if not of all the difficulty The same

transcribers. Others, such as Boston[8] and Michaelis, conclude that the original accentuators really wrote and meant to write simple R. in such cases, and that the phenomenon is not the result of error.

It is generally in verses which admit neither Athnach nor Olehveyored where this substitution occurs, though not always, lv. 23, lv. 24. It also happens that the consecution of the simple R. when substituted is the correct consecution of R. Mug. Some Edd., *e.g.* Hahn, not only substitute R. simple for R. Mug., but conversely, cxxxii. 12, xxxi. 8, xvi. 7, lxxxiii. 19. Even the compound Rbhia comes instead of the simple as its own major, xiv. 1, liii. 2.[9] These substitutions are certainly in many cases due to error, but they may be explained by supposing that between the simple and compound Rbhia there was no logical distinction, but one merely rhythmical, and that where the effect on the sense was indifferent, the ear was allowed to be the judge which accent should be employed.

view has been adopted by Baer in xviii. 1, and in the others he expunges the Zinnor entirely, although on what authority, of course, does not appear This want of citation of authority is the great defect in his beautiful edition

[8] Tractatus Stigm., p. 113.

[9] Wasmuth justly pronounces this to be *monstrum*. Mich. note in loc

§ 6. CLAUSE OF ATHNACH.

ANALYSIS

1. The ordinary servant of Athnach is Munach, ii. 1; but, *in ditione unius vocis*, that is, when there is only one word in the clause, or one word between Athnach and an accent *greater* than the minor Tippecha, the servant is Mercha, v. 9, iv. 6. Baer also points Tippecha when the accent falls on the first letter of a word.[1] Also, when Psiq is to be interposed between the words of Athnach and its servant, he still writes Mercha.[2]

2. When two words are to be connected to Athnach's word they are both pointed with Munach, ii. 4, ii. 5, ii. 11, ii. 12, etc. If Psiq be requisite before the word of Athnach, then, instead of two Munachs, Mercha and Tippecha will be employed;[3] also, according to Baer, after B. B., in two passages where is no Psiq, Job v. 27, and Job xxxiii. 31.[4] In Edd. Mercha and Tippecha will

---

[1] Tor. Em , p. 16–17. No Ed agrees with him in this, though B. B. lays down the rule expressly, this case being the *fifth* cited by him, in which the servant of Ath is Mercha, p 4–5. The others are as above

[2] Tor. Em., p 17 Though again common Edd disagree, *e g* xxxv 21, where Theile and Hahn give Munach, and so Mich

[3] Tor Em , p. 17. Ouseel, p 50. B B , p. 5.

[4] Tor Em , ibid, though Mich points these passages regularly, and

be found when there is no Psiq, *e.g.* Theile, v. 2 ; and two Munachs with Psiq.

3. If three words be connected with the word of Athnach, the words next Athnach will be punctuated with the two Munachs as in (2), and the third word will generally take Mahpach, ii. 5, vi. 6. Mahpach, however, can appear only when the accent is on the first syllable of the word, or on the second syllable, the first being a short syllable, and not having Metheg, nor commencing with Sheva,[5] xlv. 4, lxxiv. 13. Also if the accent be on the second syllable, but the first be open, the accent will still be Mahpach, which will assume Zinnorith on the open syllable,[6] or on an independent monosyllabic word, consisting of an open syllable, Job xviii. 19, Ps. cxxxvi. 4.

If the accent fall on the second syllable, the first having Metheg, or commencing with Sheva; or if the accent fall on any syllable further from the beginning than the second, the accent is Illui,[7] lx. 9, Job iv. 2.

The passage, Ps. v. 5, is thus pointed by Baer,

$$\text{כִּי׀ לֹא אֵל חָפֵץ רֶשַׁע׀אָתָּה}$$

with Psiq, and therefore Mercha Tippechatum as servant (2), and Mahpach as third servant, with Zinnorith on the open monosyllable, according to the rule given above. The confusion of Edd. on this verse is something monstrous.

Athnach has not more than three servants, except in *two*[8] passages, Ps. lcvi. 4, where there are four servants,

$$\text{כִּי גָדוֹל יְיָ וּמְהֻלָּל מְאֹד}$$

indicates no variant in his notes. But B. B. expressly excepts these two passages, and sanctions the above rule regarding the pointing with Psiq, p. 5.

[5] Tor. Ein., p. 18.

[6] Ibid, p. 19. B. B. gives the general law, that if the accent be on the first letter it will be Mahpach, otherwise Illui, p. 5.

[7] Ibid, p 18.

[8] Ibid, p. 19, according to Masor. Mich., note on the passage.

and Prov. iii. 12, where there are five, three Munachs, Mercha, and Mahpach. As to the passages, lxv. 2, lxxii. 3, Prov. i. 9, vi. 27, where Shalsheleth occurs, see § iv. 4.

4. The minor of Athnach is Dechi, ii. 1, v. 4, v. 8, vi. 4, vi. 5, vi. 7, etc. The major is Rbhia simple, ii. 7, v. 4, v. 8, vi. 2, vi. 7. Athnach may be immediately taken up by Olehveyored, the maximus of Silluq; if only one word intervene between Athnach and Oleh. that word must take a servant and not a distinctive. In three places, xlv. 8, lxviii. 5, cix. 16, Pazer occurs instead of Rbhia as major to Athnach.[9]

The minor Dechi may occur on the word next Athnach, but only if Athnach's word be long, that is, have two syllables or one long open syllable with moveable Sheva before the place of accent, xxvi. 4, xxxvii. 17, xlix. 2, etc. If, therefore, the division has to be made on the second word in Athnach's clause, Dechi can only make the division on the above conditions; if these are not present, Munach Munach must be employed. The interpunction of the clause will be :

(a) The ordinary interpunction; (b) the interpunction when distinction falls on second word, Athnach's word being long; (c) the interpunction when the distinction falls on second word, when Athnach's word is short.

---

[9] In the first two, Baer, in his Psalter, points with R. Mug. without Athnach; in the third, also without Athnach. This passage is exceedingly chaotic.

§ 7. CLAUSE OF OLEHVEYORED.

(a)

(b)

(c)

(d)

ANALYSIS.

1. Olehveyored does not occur in a clause of a single word.

(a) The normal condition of its clause is as in (a), when it consists of three or more words, with the first division on the *third* word. This division is then almost universally made by the minor Zarqa, and the second word is pointed by Galgal, the ordinary servant of Oleh., i. 1, iii. 3, iv. 7, iv. 9. It is to be observed that the minor Zinnor cannot occur without the servant Galgal, nor Galgal without Zinnor.

If the word of Oleh. be of such length that Metheg might stand on it, then Metheg may be represented by the servant Galgal, when Zinnor, of course, will follow on the *second* word, v. 11.

(b) In a very few cases Rbhia makes the distinction on the third word; Zinnor in such cases is usually present on the fourth, xxxv. 10, xlii. 5, Prov. xxx. 9.

When the distinction is made by Rbhia on the third
word, the servant of Oleh. becomes Mercha instead of
Galgal, xxxv. 10.[1] Olehveyored has never more than
one servant. According to Baer. Mahpach is servant
when such slight distinction is meant to be expressed as
is indicated by Psiq, lxxxv. 9.[2]

(c) If the clause of Oleh. consists of only one word
besides that of Oleh. itself, or if it consist of two, three
or any number of words requiring the first distinction on
the second, that distinction is almost always made by
Rbhia, ii. 7, iv. 5, iii. 6, ix. 15, lv. 13, lx. 8, xviii. 3,
ix. 21. In the majority of cases the Rbhia stands alone.
If it have a servant that servant will be Mercha, iii. 6,
xi. 6.[3] Baer asserts that if the servant's word have
Psiq, the servant is then Mahpach,[4] xx. 7, lxviii. 20,
lxxii. 19.[5]

If Rbhia have two servants, the first is Mercha and
the second is Mahpach, xx. 7, cxxxv. 6, cxxxviii. 7,
lxxii. 19, i. 2, though on the last Edd. differ. Occa-
sionally both accents may appear on the same word,
provided before the place of accent be an open syllable
formed by Qametz or Hholem, l. 3, xxvii. 11, lxviii. 36,
Job, xviii. 4.[6]

Very rarely, the distinction on the second is made by
Zinnor. In common Edd. cxl. 4, lxxviii. 38, Prov. i.

---

[1] Tor Em , p. 23   Ouseel, p. 40   Occasionally Edd write Galgal,
Theile, xlii 5 , and, curiously enough, Baer also, xxiv. 4, cii 27, in con-
tradiction to his own express rules. Spitzner would repudiate this Mercha
altogether, referring its origin to a Metheg, mistaken for Mercha.

[2] Tor. Em , p 24   Edd often write Mahpach when there is no Psiq,
Theile, xxiv. 8, lxxviii. 5, xxxi 10, vi 3, cxxxvii 7. Not so Mich , who
writes Galgal even with Psiq, repudiating Mahpach entirely, lxxxv. 9.
Not. in Ps xxiv 8.

[3] Tor. Em , p 24   Ouseel, p. 68. Ben Bilam, p 3.

[4] Edd. of course do not agree with him ; he says, however, "If you
find passages with any other servant to Rbhia, you are to know that they
are only blunders," p 24

[5] Baer cites also (Tor. Em , p. 24), xxxvi 5, but Mahp Psiq here is
rather Legarmeh, at least the passage is not one of the cases of Psiq which
he gives (Delitzsch, ii) as recognised by the Masorah.

[6] Tor. Em , p. 25.

22.   Baer agrees in cvi 47, and gives himself in addition lxxviii. 21, etc.

(d) If the clause of Olch , besides the distinction on the second word, require another distinction on the third, fourth, or fifth word, that new distinction may be made either by Zinnor or Rbhia, the distinction at the second continuing always to be made by Rbhia.   Zinnor on the third word is rare, and chiefly in these passages, xxii. 15, xxxix. 13, Prov. xxiii. 35.   Rbhia on the third, cxxxiii. 2. Zinnor on the fourth word is more common, xxvii. 9, xl. 6, xl. 15, etc.   Rbhia on the fourth is rarer, li. 6, cxliv. 13.   Zinnor on the fifth, xxviii. 7.   Rbhia on the fifth, xx. 7.

2. The minor of Oleh. is Zinnor, ni. 3, v. 7, etc.   Its usual place is on the third word, occasionally descending to the second (1 c), and occasionally ascending to the fourth, fifth, etc. (1 d).   This minor may be repeated, xvii. 14.

3. The ordinary major to Oleh. is Rbhia, i. 1, i. 3, v. 11, etc.   The older accentuists call Rbhia when immediately next Olch, Rbhia Qaton, and in any other circumstances R. Gadhol.   The consecution of both, except their servants, is the same.

§ 8. CLAUSE OF DECHI, OR TIP. ANTERIOR.

ANALYSIS.

1. Tippecha anterior stands, as its name indicates, be-
fore the first vowel of a word ; but if two words are con-
nected together by Maqqeph, it stands on the *first* word
(that nearer the *end* of the verse), though in the same
position.   It must not be supposed that this accent in-
dicates the real tone-syllable.   The invariable servant of
Dechi is Munach, i. 1, i. 5, i. 6, ii. 8, iii. 4, iv. 4, iv. 5,
etc.   If the word of Dechi have before the tone-syllable
the vowel Qamets or Hholem, and between this Qam. or
Hhol. and the tone-syllable, at least Sheva, the servant
may stand on the Qam. or Hhol. in such a way as to
seem to follow the distinctive.   (See B. B., p. 4).

2. If two words be connected together, the one next
Dechi still retains its Munach, and the second word takes
Mahpach if the accent be on the first syllable, xxxiv. 7,
xxv. 12, xxv. 6, lxxiv. 11; or if the accent be on the
second syllable, if the first be shut and not com-
mencing with Sheva, iv. 3, xxxiii. 18 ;[1] and, finally, it

[1] Tor. Em., p 21. Mich., note on iv. 3, repudiates Mahp., and seems
to consider it inadmissible unless its previous syllable can bear Zinnorith.

is still Mahp. if the accent be on the second with an open
syllable going before and not commencing with Sheva,
because then the open syllable can assume Zinnorith,
xiv. 1, liii. 2, vi. 11, Prov. xix. 24.[2] In other circum-
stances the second servant will be Illui, lxxviii. 45.

3. If three words be connected with the word of Dechi,
the first will invariably have Munach, the second Munach
or Illui, and the third Mahpach ; or if the second word
have an open syllable before the place of accent, it will
be pointed with Mahpach and Zinnorith, and then the
third will have Mercha,[3] Job xxxiv. 37.

4. The minor of Tippecha is Legarmeh, i. 5, xxxi. 3.

5. The major is Pazer, which stands occasionally on
the word next Dechi, cxxii. 4, cxxxvii. 3 ; and fre-
quently on the third word, v. 12.

[2] Tor. Em , p. 21.   Ouseel, p. 83.
[3] Tor. Em., p. 22.   Delitzsch, ii., p. 491.   Baer adds, as a reason, be-
cause two Mahpachs cannot come in close succession.   Theile, at least,
supremely contemns such narrow restrictions, v. 5, v. 10.

§ 9. CLAUSE OF ZINNOR OR ZARQA.

ANALYSIS

1. The servant of Zinnor, if the accent fall on the first letter of the word, is Mercha, i. 1, xxxii. 7 ; if the accent fall on the second letter, the first having Sheva, it is also Mercha, xxxii. 9, xlii. 10. Once more, if the accent fall on any letter of the word, if that letter bears Dagesh *forte* or *lene*, the accent is still Mercha.[1]

But if the accent fall on the second letter, the first having a vowel under it, the accent is Munach, iv. 9 ;[2] also if the accent fall on the third letter, or any higher letter being undagheshed, the accent is still Munach, xxviii. 3.[3]

If a slight distinction less than the minor be required at the servant's word, this will be indicated by Mahpach Psiq, xxxvii. 7. Prov. i. 22, though Edd. differ.[4]

---

[1] Tor. Em., p. 25 Ben Bilam, p. 2 Ouseel, 78 Ben Bilam excepts two passages, lix 1, cxvi. 6, to which Tor Em adds Job vii. 21, in which places Munach appears on a Dagheshed letter.

[2] Tor. Em., p 26. Ben Bil., p 2.

[3] Tor. Em. ut sup. Ben Bilam excepts one passage, xvii. 14, to which Tor. Em adds another, Prov. viii. 34, which are accented with Mercha on the third letter and without Daghesh.

[4] Baer cites cxviii. 27 as an example, although the passage is not one recognized by the Masorah which he produces in Delitzsch ii, containing a list of the Psiq passages in the Psalter.

2. When two words are connected before Zinnor, the one next Zinnor will have Munach or Mercha according to the rules in (1), and the second always Mahpach, i. 1. An exception is lx. 2, where two Merchas occur.[5]

3. The minor of Zinnor is Legarmeh, xxxv. 10, xl. 3, xl. 4, xl. 6, xl. 15, lxxviii. 21.

4. The major is Pazer, v. 10, xxxi. 11, xxxi. 12, xxxix. 13.

---

[5] Tor. Em., p. 27. Zinnor never has more than *two* servants. Ben Bilam, p. 1

§ 10. CLAUSE OF RBHIA.

ANALYSIS.

1. The servants of Rbhia, when immediately under Olehveyored, have been exhibited under that accent.

In other circumstances, the servant of Rbhia, if another Rbhia immediately follows, is Mercha,[1] lxxviii. 4, Prov. iv. 4.

2. When Rbhia does not follow, two cases come to be distinguished. Considering that Rbhia (when not in the immediate clause of Olehveyored) never takes more than one servant,[2] that servant must either be the first word of a clause, or be preceded immediately by Legarmeh or Pazer, the respective minor and major of Rbhia.

(a) When Legarmeh or Pazer does not precede.

   (1) If the accent falls on the second syllable, this beginning with Sheva, or if it falls on any more distant syllable, the accent is still Mercha,[3] i. 1.

   (2) If the accent falls on the first syllable or on the second, this not beginning with Sheva, then the accent is Mahpach, ii. 8, viii. 2, vi. 7.[4]

(b) But if Pazer or Legarmeh precede, then :

   (1) The accent, if it stands on a monosyllable, or

---

[1] Ouseel, p. 69. Tor. Em , p. 28.

[2] Tor. Em., p. 29, except in two cases, lv. 24, lxxxvi. 14, which common Edd. seem to increase by omitting the Psiq of Legarmeh, *e.g.* Theile, v. 3.

[3] Tor. Em., p. 28.   [4] Ibid, p. 27. B. B., p. 3.

on the second, third, etc. letter of a polysyllable, with no open syllable before the tone, is Illui,[5] i. 3, ii. 12, v. 3, v. 9, xl. 13, xlv. 3, xlv. 5, lx. 9, lx. 10.

(2) But if the word be not monosyllabic, and have the accent on the first syllable, the accent is then Mahpach, xciii. 4; or if the accent be not on the first, with an open syllable before it, the open syllable may take Zinnorith and the other Mahpach,[6] iv. 2.

3. The minor to Rbhia is Legarmeh. i. 3, ii. 12, iv. 2, x. 21, xxv. 7, lx. 8, lxiii. 2, lxxiii. 28, lxxxvii. 4. etc.

4. The major to Rbhia is Pazer, ii. 12, iv. 2, xiii. 3, .xxii. 5, etc.

---

[5] Tor. Em., p. 28. Ben Bilam, p. 3.   [6] Tor. Em., p. 29.

§ 11. CLAUSE OF PAZER.

ANALYSIS.

1. The servant of Pazer is Galgal, v. 12. If the word of Pazer be of such a length that Metheg might have also stood on it, Galgal may take the place of Metheg, xxxii. 5.[1]

According to Baer, if a slight pause requiring Psiq occur, Mahpach is used along with it,[2] xlv. 8, Prov. xxx. 8, Ps 1. 1, lix. 6, cxli. 4.

2. If two words be connected together before Pazer, the first takes Galgal and the second Mahpach if the accent be on the first syllable of the word, v. 10, but Azla if not, v. 12.[3]

3. When three words stand connected before Pazer, the third has Mahpach, the second Qadma, and the one next Pazer, Galgal, or Mahpach Psiq, xxiii. 4. Often Edd. give Mahp. without Psiq, xxii. 25. Pazer has never more than three servants.[4]

4. The minor of Pazer is Legarmeh, vii. 6, xix. 15.

---

[1] Mich. writes Mahpach here, and charges MSS and Edd with writing "Jerach pro Mahp. *irregulariter*." See note 3 below. Theile actually prints *Munach*.

[2] Tor. Em., p 29

[3] Ibid. The rule given by Spitzner, Institutions, p 231, on the authority of Mich. is, that if Mahpach be on the third word, Galgal is servant; but if Azla be on the third word, Mahpach is servant. The confusion in Edd here is monstrous. Mich. points according to his own rule. Ben Bilam lays down a rule differing from any of the above.

[4] Ben Bilam, p 1.

§ 12. CLAUSE OF LEGARMEH.

ꞮꞮ— (no serv)   Ꞇ   Ꞇ— (repetitus),

ꞮꞮ—   Ꞇ   Ꞇ— etc, (repet.)

ANALYSIS

1. If Legarmeh has another word in connection with it, so as to want a servant, Azla Legar. must be employed.[1]

2. If Legarmeh occur in the clause of Silluq, it is always Mahpach Leg., except cxxv. 3, a passage otherwise irregular, and a few more.[2]

3. When Legarmeh requires no servant, and is not in the clause of Silluq, either Mahp. Leg. or Azla Leg. may be employed, though not indifferently. The rules given by Baer are somewhat subtle, and by no means conformed to in Edd.

(a) If the accent stand on the first syllable of a word, Mah. Leg. is to be expected, xxiii. 6. xxiv. 4, xxxii. 4, xxvii. 8.[3]

Also, if the accent is on the second syllable, if the first letter of that syllable have Sheva or Dagesh, it is still Mahp. Legar, xliv. 3, i. 5, xxi. 5, xxii. 28, xxxi. 15, lxxiii. 28, xiii. 6, xv. 5, xxxii. 7.

[1] This general law was known even to Spitzner and Ouseel

[2] The rule is generally adhered to by Edd., and declared to be without exception by Baer. Mich writes Azla Leg, lxii. 13 , probably, as Azla is second servant in Silluq's clause, the Psiq should be excided.

[3] This rule was recognised by the older accentuists, though not without exception Mich gives Azla Leg on first syllable, lvi. 10, xliv. 3, etc.

Once more, if the accent be on the second syllable, and the first be an open syllable not beginning with Sheva, the accent is Mah. Legarmeh, x. 7, xvi. 9, lxxiii. 8, lxxiii. 10, xxvii. 4.

(*b*) If the accent stands on second syllable, the first beginning with Sheva, then Azla Legarm. is used, xxvi. 1, xxvii. 1, xxi. 10,[4] xxviii. 7, v. 9, xli. 3. So Azla Legarm. is used if the accent be on the third syllable or nearer the end, xci. 4, cxi. 1, lxvi. 4,[5] lxix. 16, xviii. 7, xxxi. 21, xxxii. 9, cix. 14, xcviii. 1, xxxi. 12, lx. 2, etc.

4. The servant of Legarmeh (always Azla Legar.) is sometimes Mahpach, sometimes Illui, sometimes Mahp. with Zinnorith.[6] Baer, pp. 32–34 of his treatise, lays down very minute rules, the substance of which is, that if the accent fall on the first letter of the word it is Mahpach; or on the second letter, the first having Sheva, it is still Mahpach; or if it fall on the second syllable, the first ending with Sheva quiescent or Dag. (*i.e.* being *shut*), the accent is also Mahpach (pp. 32-33). Also, if the accent fall on the second syllable, or farther; or anywhere, with an open syllable immediately before the tone, whether the open syllable be part of the same word, or an independent monosyllable, the accent is still Mahpach, and the open syllable has Zinnorith (p. 34).

If these conditions are not conformed to, the accent is Illui (p. 33).

Legarmeh has no more than one servant except in two places, cxvii. 2, cxliii. 3, where the second servant is Mercha.[7]

5. The minor of Legarmeh is Legarmeh. Perhaps it

---

[4] But Mich. prints Mahp Legarmeh here, so Theile So both give Mahp. Leg. on the three next cited passages

[5] Mich. however points this passage with Mahp. Leg on third syllable and so the next four cited passages , so cix. 14.

[6] B. B. leaves the thing in this indefinite state, p. 3, 4.

[7] According to the express dictum of the Masorah on the latter passage. Mich. not in loc , who adds another passage on the authority of the Masorah, viz , xcvi. 4 See clause of Athnach For the Azla in Prov. xxiv. 31, Baer would read Pazer.

would be better to say, Legarmeh may be repeated. The rules applying to the accent itself, apply to the accent repeated, xxvii. 1, xxxii. 4, xxvi. 1. An instructive passage is xlii. 5, cxliv. 1.

Note.—It is better to write the verses beginning הַלְלוּ יָהּ, which have Legarmeh on the יָהּ, as one word הַלְלוּיָהּ׀ with Mich. and Baer, instead of putting Azla Leg. irregularly on the *yah*, and Mercha also irregularly on the *halelu*, as is done by common Edd., Ps. cxlvii. 1, cxlviii. 1, cxlix. 1, cl. 1, cxxxv. 1, cxiii. 1, cxii. 1 ; and sanctioned by Ouseel, p. 98.

THE END.

CPSIA information can be obtained
at www.ICGtesting.com
Printed in the USA
BVHW040046250620
582286BV00005B/160